Songs of Rebirth

Scores, Leadsheets, and Transcriptions from the Album

Jeremy Siskind

Cover Art by Nancy Harms
Cover Design by Sofia Tendeiro
Transcriptions by Eric Bell

ISBN 978-1-7351695-6-9

Visit Jeremy Siskind online at www.jeremysiskind.com

Table of Contents

About *Songs of Rebirth*

It's no secret that 2020 was a year of tearing down. So many assumptions, structures, careers, relationships, and routines ended as the pandemic razed the foundations on which they were built.

The years ahead of us present an unparalleled opportunity for rebuilding. As individuals and as a society, we will get to decide how we will emerge from the rubble and what kinds of new structures we will erect.

Like so many others, my personal life went through a massive upheaval during the pandemic. When my long-term relationship ended, I "started over" in a new home and new city and with the challenge of reenvisioning my identity from scratch. It felt threatening but also deeply hopeful. It's been hard but also energizing.

All this led me to contemplate rebirth, both for myself and for the world. Is rebirth even possible? How can it be approached with intention? What conditions facilitate a reawakening? How can a person or society make a purposeful change instead of sleepwalking through an unintentional evolution (or devolution)?

The songs on this album are meditations on these questions and representations of rebirth stories in art, science, philosophy, psychology, and culture. Some are personal and some are grandiose. Some are serious and some are silly.

The two discs have different themes. The songs on the first disc represent successful rebirthings where a character reemerges meaningfully transformed. On the second disc, the characters mostly fail at their attempts to remake themselves or others. As the "comic relief," I've interwoven verses from a vaudeville-esque song I wrote called "I'd Break Quarantine for You" throughout the two discs. Each verse is set in a different music style with the hopes of delighting the listener and cleansing their palette between pieces.

Special thanks are due to my trio mates, Nancy Harms and Lucas Pino as well as to our recording engineer and spiritual guide, Tom Zink. It's been rewarding seeing both members of my ensemble being "reborn" in their own ways during the recording process. During the pandemic, Nancy became a serious painter and is responsible for the album's beautiful cover art and disc art. And Lucas became a father! Bryna Gardenia Pino was born in August of 2021. For me, among other transformations, I started writing and self-publishing books, and I decided that it would be appropriate to present this music in book form as well. Now that you're reading this book, you're part of my rebirth story!

Sincere thanks for checking out this music!

Jeremy Siskind, 2022

Notes on the Book

Thank you for your interest in the music from *Songs of Rebirth*. I'm proud of this music and I hope it doesn't only entertain and move you, but that it also prompts you to think about how you want to show up in the world in the next few years.

A few notes about what you're seeing:

- These charts are very close to the ones we brought into the studio. In some cases, they're "cleaned up" to make them more attractive on the page. In other cases, they've been re-written to reflect what we ended up recording. I haven't gone back and tried to write down improvised introductions, endings, or solos. Hopefully, it's interesting to be able to see what was through-composed and what was invented on the spot.
- While composing this set of music, I frequently heard melodies and chords that don't quite match. Although typos are always possible, most of these chords are *not* typos, even if they seem mismatched with the melody. I wasn't fastidious about accounting for every single alteration or non-chord tone. I simply wrote these down the way I heard them.
- Some of these pieces are highly through-composed. Where there's a completely written-out section ("Reincarnation," "We Will Not Go Back to Normal") I've provided it just as we read it in the studio.
- All of these charts are in concert pitch, even pieces where a clarinet or saxophone part is notated. I can provide transposed charts upon request.

Notes on the Songs

I'd Given Up
I scratched down these lyrics sometime in the mid-2010s at the 55 Bar in New York City while listening to vocalist Kate McGarry and guitarist Keith Ganz. Their performance was so mesmerizing that it conquered my cynicism. This song is unique in my experience because it states the same short poem four times in a row with very different musical settings.

I chose to make this the first song on the album because it feels like an invocation for what our ensemble is trying to do through music. We want to use the power of art to change a life. "I'd Given Up" is also a challenge to the listener to step outside of their own cynicism and to be open to letting art affect you.

There are no improvised solos on this piece. The second time through, the melody is re-stated in alternating phrases between the solo clarinet and the piano and voice presenting the melody in unison.

Unbroken String
The seed of this lyric was planted in Marilynne Robinson's book, *Lila*. Ironically, the part that inspired me was from a "bad" poem that a character wrote as a gift to another character (the character who wrote the poem bemoans the fact that "trembling" is really two syllables, but rhythmically takes up three).

Still, I found the poem really intriguing. "Had my heart an unbroken string/your touch would send it trembling" seems to imply that the heart's strings are all broken and therefore love is hopeless. However, the fact that one would even imagine their heartstrings trembling means that there is hope, however frightening it may be. I took this seed and expanded it to three verses, putting a bass ostinato and solos in between.

In Every Moment
"In Every Moment" was inspired by a Rumi poem that I've seen titled "No End to the Journey." The poem is metaphysical, romantic, and at least a little erotic. It speaks of love as "dying into" another person, being "reborn" through the union. It encourages a lover to "take an axe to the prison wall" of reality. There's something about the poem that feels "realer than real."

I attempted to capture this heightened state with technicolor chords. There are many heightened dissonances, triads stacked over other triads, and wild swings in harmony, relying on Lucas' muscular saxophone playing to tie the disparate sounds together. Here, we expand a locrian pedal for Lucas to improvise freely, coming briefly "unmoored" from time and space.

I'd Break Quarantine for You, Verse 1
This series started as a lark. What kind of a love song would fit with the pandemic? Well, maybe an attraction too great for even a lockdown to hold it back! It seemed only fitting to write this in a classic Broadway/vaudeville style to lampoon the idea of a "timeless" love song being stuck in a very specific place and time.

I decided to separate the verses to create a serial story throughout the album. We interpreted each in a different musical style for variety and good fun. The styles are the sugar that helps the "medicine" go down easier.

Lethe-Reincarnation
This "medley" started out as two separate pieces which felt destined to come together. I wrote "Lethe" while considering Lewis Hyde's book, *A Primer on Forgetting*, which explains that in many mythological traditions before one can be reborn, she must be cleared of all her old memories. In this song, a character reflects on their most treasured memories and decides that they must be sacrificed in exchange for another shot at life.

The second half is one of the more through-composed pieces of the set. Like "In Every Moment," I set out to write a piece that captured the metaphysical feeling of being reborn. The piece that follows feels to me like a magical musical stew being stirred vigorously together. I imagine the repeated notes as the moments where the transfiguration is taking place and the final section where the voice "breaks free" of the piano as the moment of seeing sunlight again in a new body. Yes, there is a held G natural against an F-sharp major chord on purpose!

Drinking Song
The lyric for "Drinking Song" is taken from compiled quotes from Charles Bukowski, who was fond of describing drinking as a kind of rebirth. The music bares inspiration from the Fred Hersch/Norma Winstone piece "Procrastination," which also mixes elements of stride and boogie-woogie piano with some Monk-like in-the-cracks melodic choices and a semi-sarcastic tone. When singing, hold the "ay" in "away" long enough to allow it to become the first "A" in "Aviator gin."

Serotiny
Originally entitled "Fire," this song is about serotinous plants. These plants release their seeds only in extreme heat, usually when a fire is burning. I learned about these plants from a podcast featuring poet-activist Terry Tempest Williams. Remarkably, serotinous are often *already* revegetating the land by the time a fire's finished burning. What a beautiful metaphor for a reawakening!

"Serotiny" was written during one of the periods in September 2021 when southern California was enveloped in smoke and orange sky and I was stuck inside, surrounded by the alien light of a blood red sun. As much as the piece is about the hope of rebirth, it's also written as an elegy for the American West.

I'd Break Quarantine, vol. 2
There's not much more to say about this, except to note that this piece was written and recorded *before* any of the Cuomo scandals broke. For better or for worse, the governor's name meant something quite different than it does now. I still think it's a fun rhyme!

Kneel
"Kneel" is the only song on the album that wasn't written during the pandemic period. The trio has performed "Kneel" for almost ten years, but it's never been properly recorded. It seemed to match the theme of the album beautifully because it speaks about the power and possibility of spiritual renewal.

Derek Walcott's biography, *Another Life*, inspired this lyric. Walcott, a St. Lucian poet, writes about a moment in which he simultaneously comprehends the beauty of his home in the Caribbean and the suffering and poverty of its inhabitants. Trying to hold these two ideas together in his mind overwhelms him and he falls to his knees in conscious or unconscious prayer. He has no choice but to submit to some sort of higher authority when faced with the question of how so much beauty and so much suffering can coexist.

The improvisation here is a free improvisation. There was no real prompt except maybe the idea of the "innocence" of the "schoolgirl in blue and white" and the "kiss by the boathouse door" that are mentioned in the lyric. As with many elements of this album, I owe a great deal of gratitude and influence here to John Taylor and Tony Coe. Here, I was thinking about their instrumental improvisation on the piece "Somewhere Called Home" from the Norma Winstone album of the same name.

So I Went to New York City to Be Born Again

The titular phrase is taken from a passage from Kurt Vonnegut's novel *Bluebeard*. Regardless of the specifics of the novel, there's something about picking up and moving to New York that feels like a vital human experience. Everybody in my trio has done it at some point. There's a faith in moving to New York which reflects a dedication to pursuing something important, something big, something pure.

Musically, this is one of the more "straight-ahead" jazz pieces on the album. I don't know if anybody else would recognize this influence, but I was thinking of some of Ornette Coleman's melodies that have a singable tune but unexpected chords. The chords written as triads are really triads.

In this chart, I included the notated "head out" with a second lyric, even though we didn't end up including that portion in the final recording. The ending of the solo section ended up being a really effective transition into the next song, so we just omitted the final "verse" of lyrics. That's how it goes in the studio sometimes!

New

"New" is a love song! Actually, it wasn't originally a love song – it went through quite a few different lyrical identities before it arrived at this version, but I think it finally found its voice. Here, the interlude was inspired by Fred Hersch's "A Riddle Song," particularly the way it was orchestrated on *Fred Hersch Trio + 2*. I decided to take a piano solo before the first melody to do something a little different and in tribute to/imitation of John Taylor/Norma Winstone's version of "Strange Meadowlark."

The lyric for "New" feels more personal than literary. As the pandemic began, I got out of a long-term relationship. In that situation, I found it difficult to see my way back to joy, love, and belonging. And yet, the world has a way of surprising you and making you new again.

We Will Not Go Back to Normal

Inspired by a quote from Sonya Renée Taylor, "We Will Not Go Back to Normal" refers to the desire to make something *better* out of society after the pandemic, not merely return to our old ways. Ms. Taylor encourages us to all "stitch a new garment." The piece itself is a new garment, a musical experiment. The three instruments play as a true chamber trio, fully notated, with the piano only playing one note at a time. It was a challenge to get voice, piano, and bass clarinet to match tone, dynamic and pitch, but I think we got a nice recording! The music borders on Copland-esque, but I found myself working to resist the "fanfare Americana" genre that would be easy to fall into here.

Growing Pains

A wordless composition, "Growing Pains" was inspired by personal experience and the Iron and Wine lyric, "there's no way to grow that don't hurt." Lucas plays a beautiful free introduction on this piece and plays a pretty epic solo on the final vamp before the fade. The final vamp is the only place on the album where we (briefly) overdub Nancy. If you listen closely, you can hear her singing in octaves to support Lucas' solo over this undulating, back-and-forth ostinato.

It's ultimately this back-and-forthness that the tune is really about. On one hand, as humans, we seek growth, healing, and new pastures. On the other hand, confronting the discomfort that comes with growth can be deeply stressful and terrifying. How we figure out the balance between challenging ourselves and seeking comfort is one of the great mysteries and struggles of being human.

I'd Break Quarantine for You, Verse 3

As I confronted this strange tune I'd written, "I'd Break Quarantine for You," I started to ask myself if it was immoral. There are many songs celebrating lust, but risking your life and others' for lust? At best it seemed not too funny. At worst it seemed downright crude.

You can hear some hints in this verse about the turn that the story is starting to take. I arranged this verse for four wind instruments – two clarinets and two bass clarinets – to provide a really big change of pace from the piano-drenched texture on the rest of the album.

Long Beach, in Fog

"Long Beach, in Fog" is part of my personal rebirth story. Midway through the pandemic, I essentially "started over." I ended a long-term relationship, moved out of the house I'd been sharing with my partner in Orange County, and moved to Long Beach, near the ocean. Immediately, in this new setting and new reality, I felt a shift starting to take place. I felt more free, more independent, and more like myself. In those early days, my neighborhood would frequently be ensconced in thick fog, which added a magical majesty to the long walks I'd take among the old bungalows, contemplating the possibilities that spread out in front of me.

New Year, New You

Written in celebration of New Years Day 2021, this piece mocks the idea of new year's resolutions or, at least, the thought that you can change your habits in the carefree way that the mass media is convincing us you should. Even though this song is very cynical, I actually think it's optimistic. The lyric suggests that change is accomplished through hard, intentional work over a long period of time, not by a sudden shift based on a randomly chosen date.

Musically, I've been told that this piece sounds related to Bernstein's *West Side Story*, particularly the song "Cool." It does have some of the same roots – a pulsating Charleston rhythm, chords with tritone bass movements, and a short, clipped melody. It separates itself, potentially, through its use of odd tuplets and a virtuosic line shared by the saxophone and piano.

The whole tune sets up the joke at the very end, in which the narrator says, "each year, I still try." The last line admits that although we all know, on some level, that some things are scams, it's only human to want an easy fix.

I'd Break Quarantine for You, Verse 4

Here, things start to go wrong in this Quarantineland. Although the couple finally consummated their love, they're learning that actions have consequences. On the album, we performed this one as a slow tango, ironically matching the most romantic style with the least romantic verse…so far.

April, the Liar

Edna St. Vincent Millay wrote a brilliant poem called "Spring" that "April, the Liar" works to capture through music. Millay destroys the poetic trope of spring bringing rebirth each year. Instead, she asserts that although "it is apparent that there is no death," "underground are the brains of men being eaten by maggots" and "April comes like an idiot, babbling and strewing flowers." Ah! Time isn't cyclical, it's linear! The poets have duping us all along! I loved this idea and I also loved being able to make Nancy sing the lyric "we're all gonna die/ April's a lie."

Demeter

The story of Demeter and Persephone is one of the most important rebirth myths in Western civilization. My song, "Demeter," is based on a beautiful poem by British poet Carol Ann Duffy, who writes the story of Demeter not as a goddess but as a mother for whom her daughter's absence is deeply personal. In fact, I think many of us experience a sort of rebirth when we're around our distant family, friends, or loved ones.

The bare harmony of the opening reflects the barren, primitive landscape described in Duffy's poem. The middle section is an outgrowth of my work with the perpetual motion style, as reflected most prominently in my *Perpetual Motion Etudes*. There's something chant-like about the line that I wrote for voice and clarinet together to sing over the pulsating piano part. It sounds roughly Scandinavian and makes me think of Vikings for reasons I couldn't begin to guess.

I'd Break Quarantine for You, Verse 5

Note that the end of the saga, the character chooses to place blame elsewhere, reversing "I'd break quarantine for you" to become "when *you* broke quarantine for *me*." We chose to perform this verse in a way that contrasts with the narrative to avoid become too maudlin or overly dramatic.

Forgiveness

I wrote this piece because I wanted to include something that resembled the version of "Whispering Grass" that my trio performed on the album *Housewarming*. In this piece, the bass clarinet takes on the role of bass and frees up the piano to play in the upper register. This requires so much constant playing from the bass clarinet that poor Lucas was really out of breath by the time the track was done!

The interlude is interesting from an arranging perspective. I wanted the voice to be the middle part between two piano notes, so my chords surround Nancy as she sings her line. It's quite hard to execute both pianistically and vocally because we're so used to having the melody on top. The voicings used mostly have a second on bottom and a fifth on top.

"Forgiveness" can often represent the rebirth of a relationship. I was inspired to write the song after listening to psychologist Harriet Lerner talk to Brené Brown about the art of apologizing and forgiving on a podcast. In the last verse, we learn that this person is no longer around to accept an apology and forgiveness is impossible.

Another Birthday

I'm grateful for birthday celebrations, but the older I get, the more ornery I get whenever my birthday rolls around (October 14, if you want to send a gift!). This song presents my internal dialogue leading up to my birthday celebration with some extra comedy sprinkled on top. Although I'd originally envisioned Lucas playing saxophone, he insisted that clarinet was the right choice and imagine this as something you might hear in a Woody Allen movie. I think he made the right call, and he plays a beautiful solo that captures my feeling of ambivalence.

Disc 1 Leadsheets and Scores

I'd Given Up

Jeremy Siskind

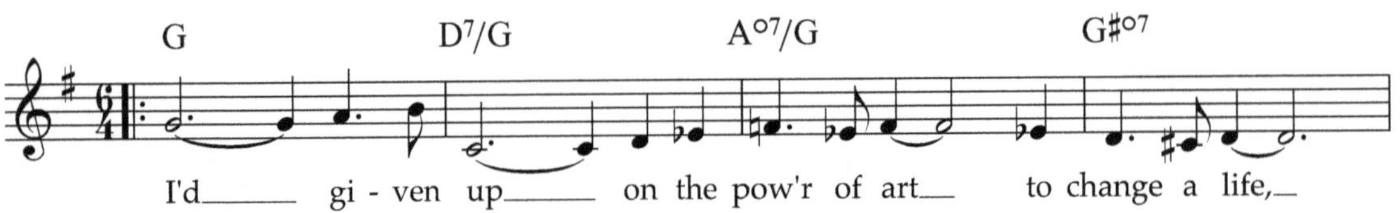

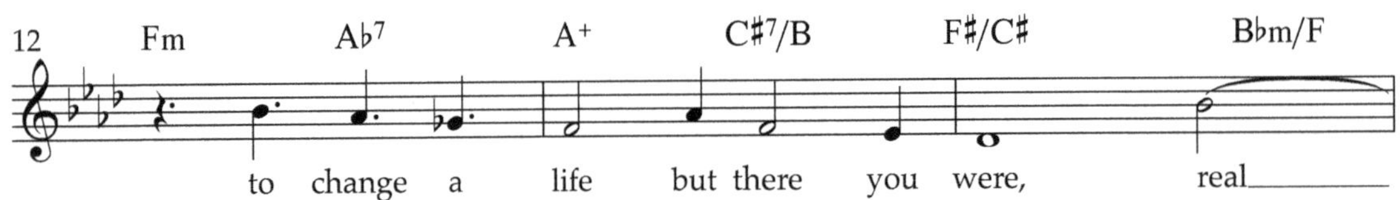

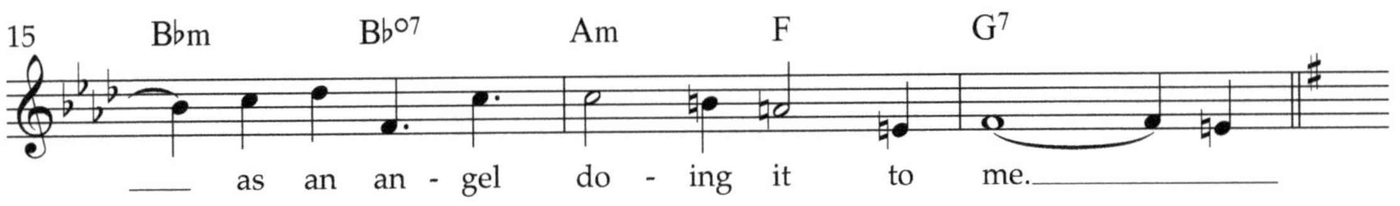

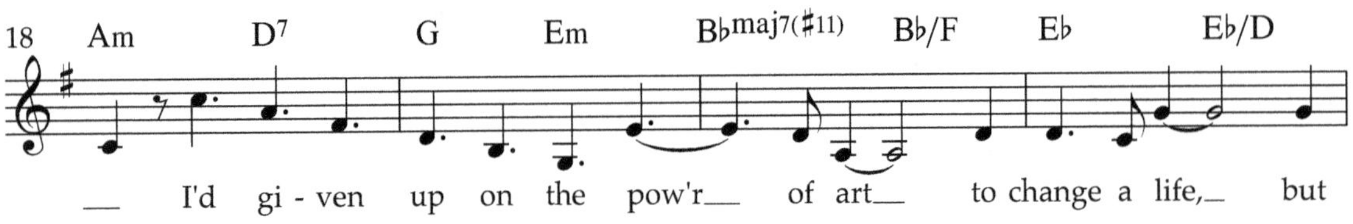

22
D♭ D♭/C B♭m E♭7 A♭ D♭
3
3
there you were,_ real as an an - gel, do - ing it to me.

25
B♭m E♭7 E♭7/D♭ A♭/C D♭ B♭7/D E♭ E
I'd gi-ven up on the po-wer of art to change a life,___ but there you

29
C♯m/C B7alt. D7alt.
were, real as an an - gel___ do - ing it to

Coda
32
G F♯/G
me.

34
F♯/D F/C Dm

36
A♭ C/G Em Gm G♭ D/E♭

40
G
42
G
44
G
F#/D
G
F#/D
G

Unbroken String

Jeremy Siskind

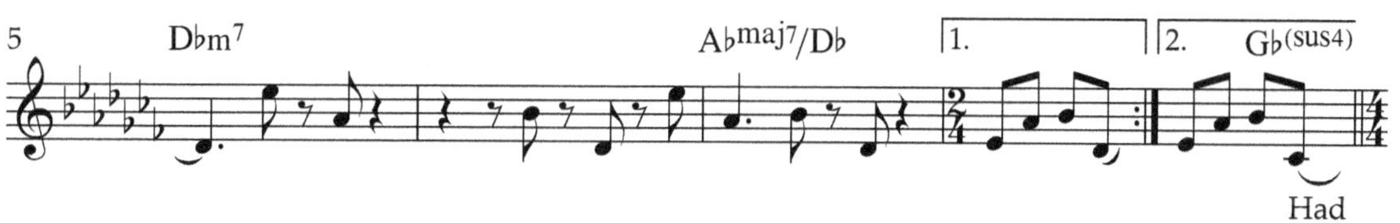

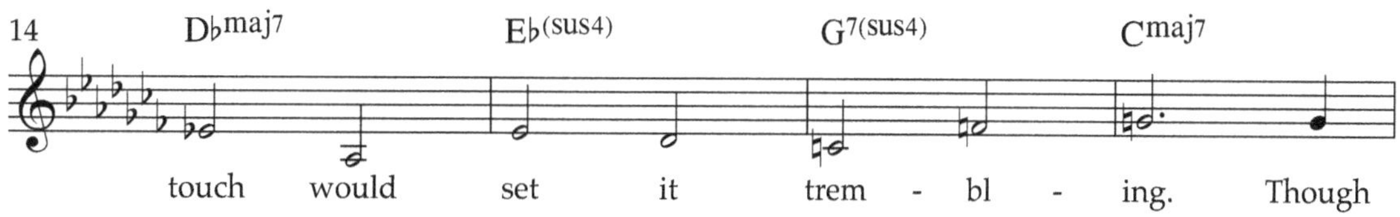

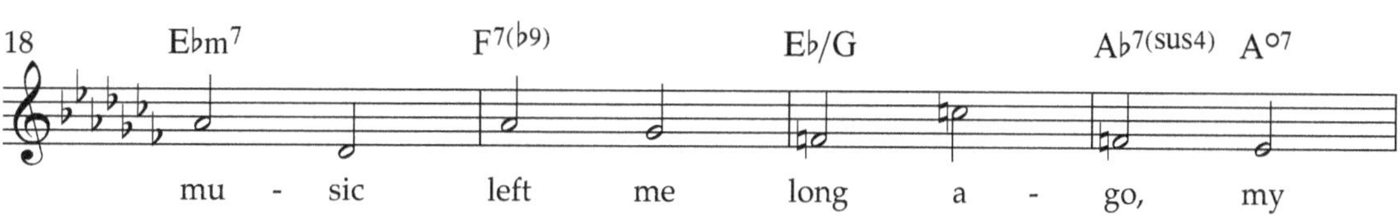

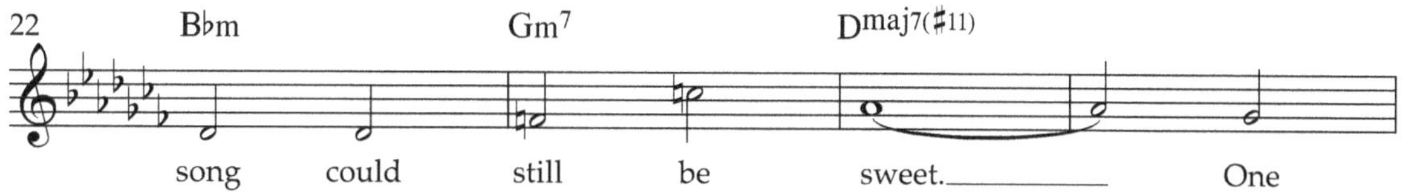

26
G♭maj7/B♭ Gmaj7/B Dm7
touch would set me trem - bl - ing, and
30
Amaj7 A♭/C
start my heart to
32
D♭m7 D♭maj7
beat.
36
D♭m7 A♭maj7/D♭
1.
2. G♭(sus4)
Had
41
G♭(sus4) A♭/C B♭/D Amaj7
— my heart an un - clipped wing, your
45
D♭maj7 E♭(sus4) G7(sus4) Cmaj7
smile would start it flut - ter - ing. Though
49
E♭m7 F7(♭9) E♭/G A♭7(sus4) A°7
I was groun - ded long a - go, I
53
B♭m Gm7 Dmaj7(♯11)
dream of o - pen sky. Your

57
G♭maj7/B♭
Gmaj7/B
Dm7
Amaj7
A♭/C
smile could mend my bro - ken wings, one smile and I could
Lead Into Solos
63
D♭m7
D♭maj7
fly.
67
D♭m7
A♭maj7/D♭
1.
2.
G♭(sus4)
Solos
72
G♭(sus4)
A♭/C
B♭/D
Amaj7
76
D♭maj7
E♭(sus4)
G7(sus4)
Cmaj7
80
E♭m7
F7(♭9)
E♭/G
A♭7(sus4)
A○7
84
B♭m
Gm7
Dmaj7(♯11)
G♭maj7/B♭
89
Gmaj7/B
Dm7
Amaj7
A♭/C

On Cue
94
D♭m7
D♭maj7
98
D♭m7
A♭maj7
1.
2.
G♭(sus4)
Had
103
G♭(sus4)
A♭/C
B♭/D
Amaj7
— my heart a stur - dy oar, your
107
D♭maj7
E♭(sus4)
G7(sus4)
Cmaj7
kiss would launch me from the shore. Though
111
E♭m7
F7(♭9)
E♭/G
A♭7(sus4)
A°7
I've been land - locked 'lo these years, I
115
B♭m
Gm7
Dmaj7(♯11)
crave the o - cean's spray.
119
G♭maj7/B♭
Gmaj7/B
Dm7
If you kissed me, dear, my
123
Amaj7
A♭/C
heart could sail a

Vamp Until Cue
125
D♭m7
D♭maj7
way.
129
D♭m7
A♭maj7/D♭
1.
2.
D♭m7

In Every Moment

Jeremy Siskind

30
Am F/E♭ Emaj7 D7/B♭ D♭maj7 Bmaj7/G E♭m/G♭
34
B♭/D F♯ Dm/A C♯ E/G♯
(piano)
38
B♭ D♭ Em B♭ D♭ Em
42
B♭ D♭ Gm A
fine
Vocals
46
C♯m/E Bm7/F♯ C♯m/E
Hold me this mid-win-ter's night. E-ven li - lac trees wear their wed-ding gowns.
50
Dmaj7 C♯m/D♯
Time does-n't ex - ist. For
54
Amaj7/D Dmaj7/G♯ E/C♯ D♯ø7
as we kiss, the se - conds breed per - pet - u - al in - fin - i - ties. Our
58
E6 B A/C♯
souls were born to har-mo-nize e - ter-nal-ly. I will

62 G/B Am/C Bb/D G#7/D# C#m/E C#m6
4 4 4
die in to your arms this night with faith I'll feel the

65 E/D# E7(sus4) Amaj7/C#
sun as it shines out your soul. I know I will. Our

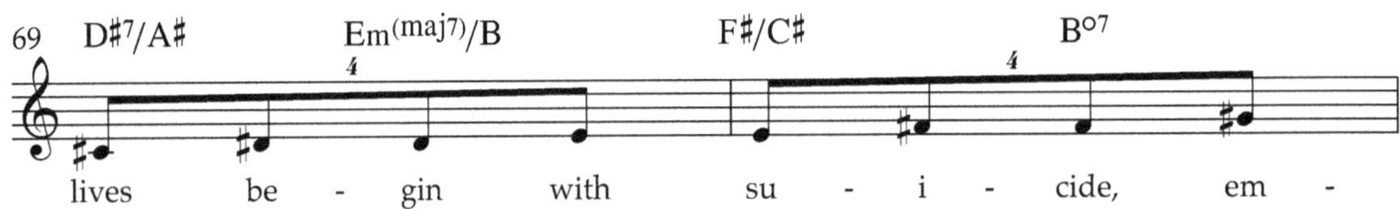
69 D#7/A# Em(maj7)/B F#/C# B°7
4 4
lives be - gin with su - i - cide, em -

71 A#+ D/A Amaj7/D# G7(#11)
brace me and be born a - gain in

73 F#7(sus4) G#/F# Em/F# G#/F#
show-ers of tur-quoise and gold.
(saxophone)

77 A/G D#ø7/F# G#°7 A
3
Die in-to me now, my love.
D.C. al fine

I'd Break Quarantine for You

Jeremy Siskind

Lethe-Reincarnation

Jeremy Siskind

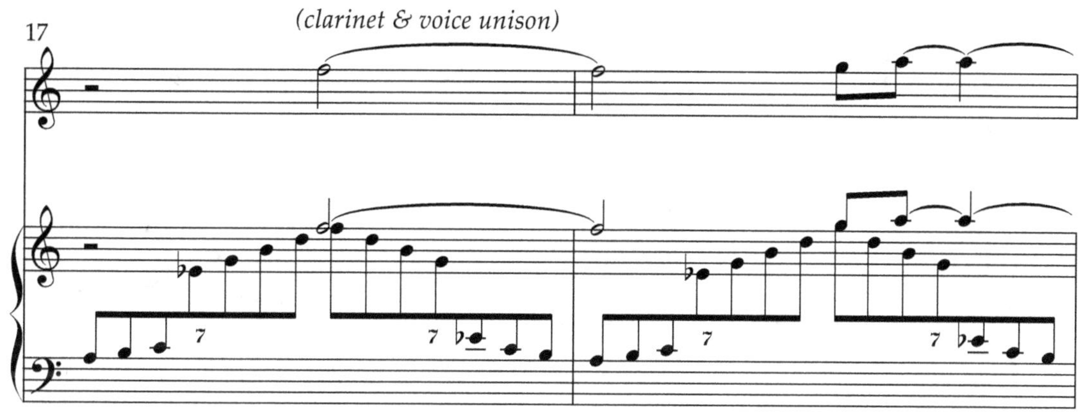
17
(clarinet & voice unison)
7
7
7
7

19
7
7
7
7

21
3
3
7
7
7
7

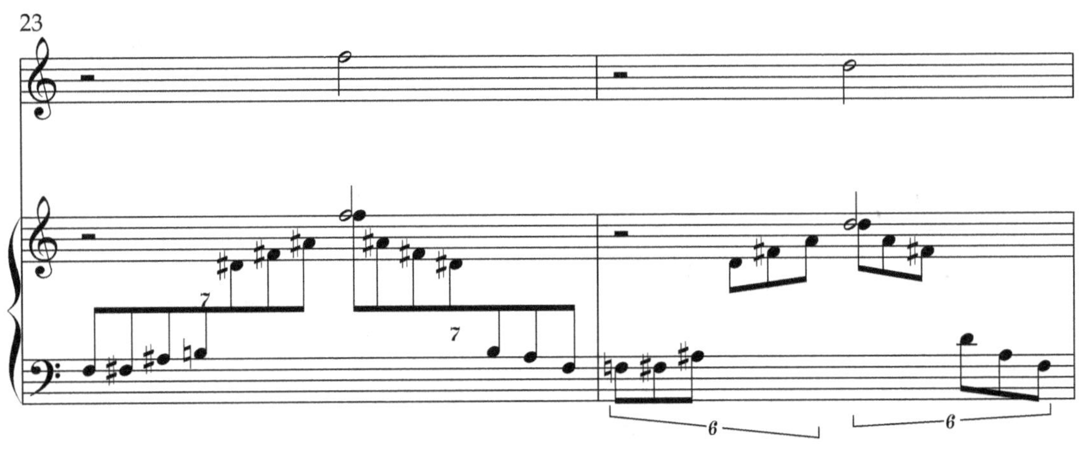
23
7
7
6
6

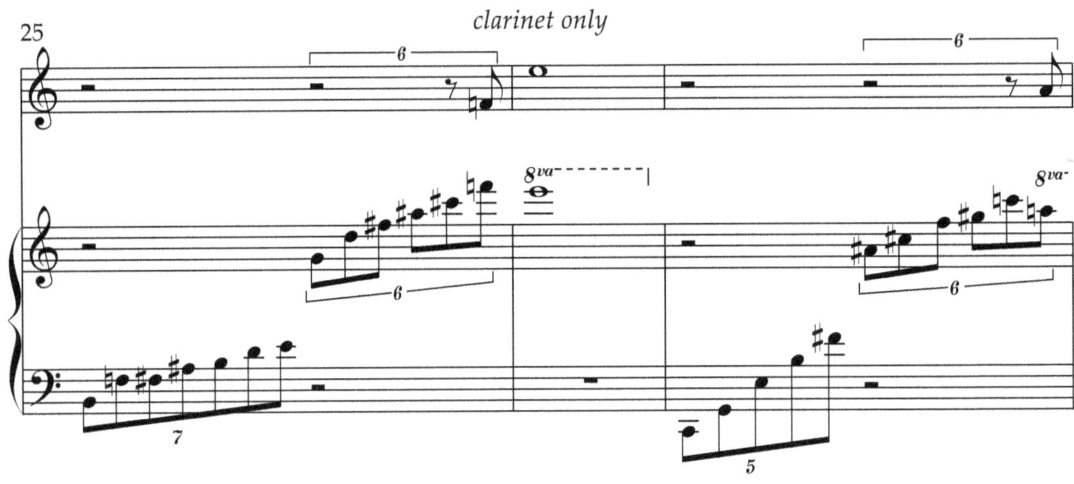
clarinet only
25
6
6
8va
6
8va
6
7
5

28
(8)
8va
6
7

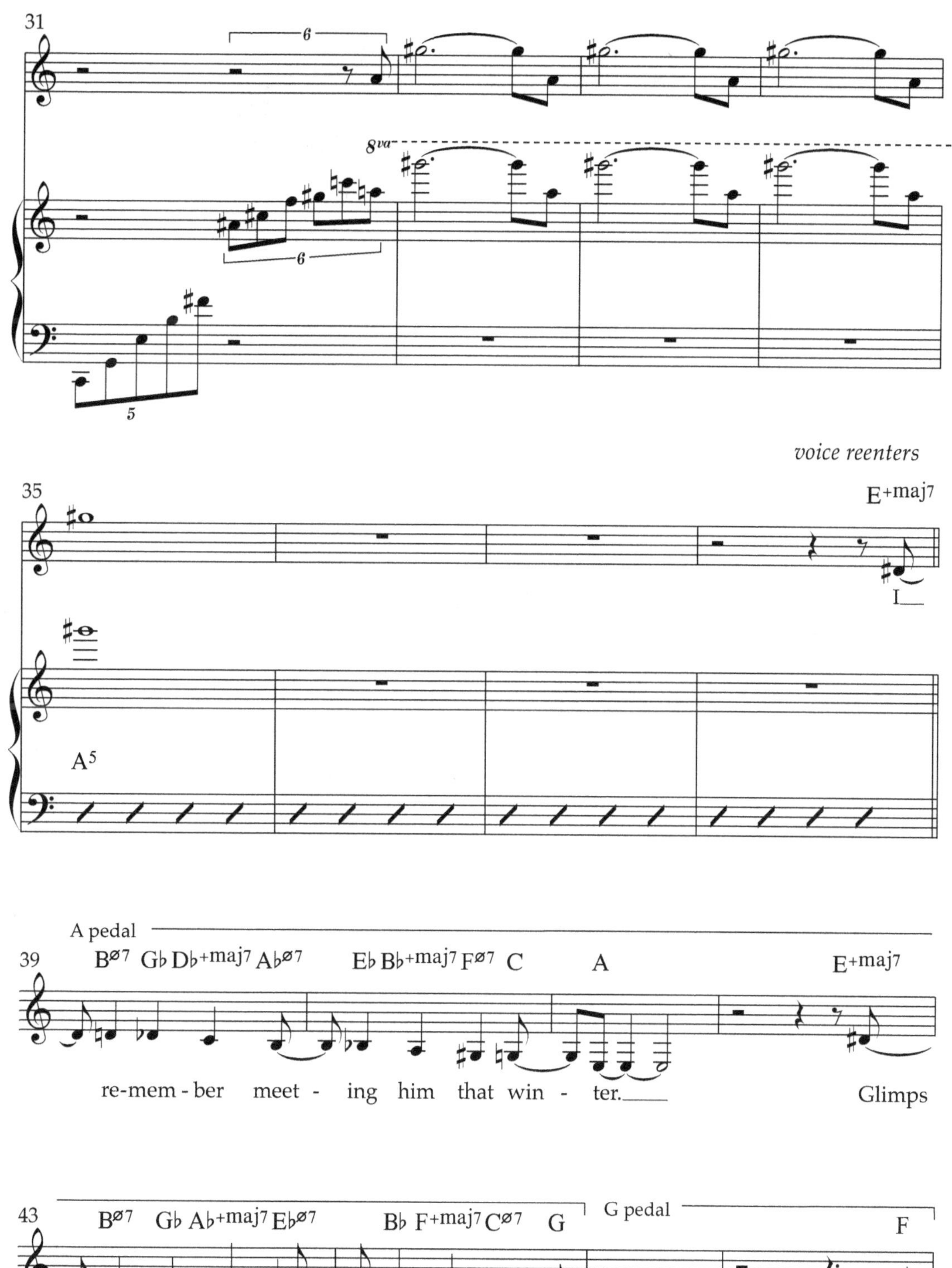
31
6
8va
6
5
voice reenters
35
E+maj7
I
A5
A pedal
39
B∅7 G♭ D♭+maj7 A♭∅7
E♭ B♭+maj7 F∅7 C
A
E+maj7
re-mem-ber meet - ing him that win - ter.
Glimps
43
B∅7 G♭ A♭+maj7 E♭∅7
B♭ F+maj7 C∅7 G
G pedal
F
- ing some-thing spec - ial in his eyes.
Ev-

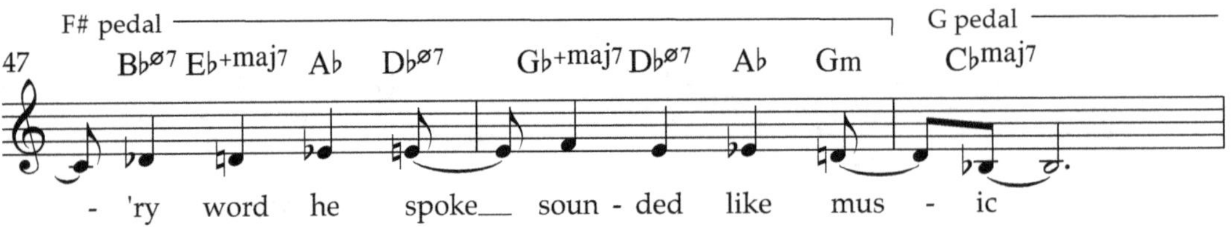
F# pedal
G pedal
47
B♭ø7 E♭+maj7 A♭ D♭ø7 G♭+maj7 D♭ø7 A♭ Gm C♭maj7
- 'ry word he spoke soun - ded like mus - ic

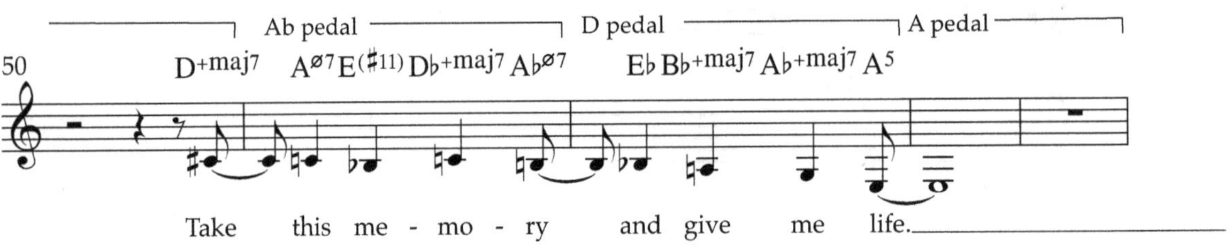
Ab pedal
D pedal
A pedal
50
D+maj7 Aø7 E(♯11) D♭+maj7 A♭ø7 E♭ B♭+maj7 A♭+maj7 A5
Take this me - mo - ry and give me life.

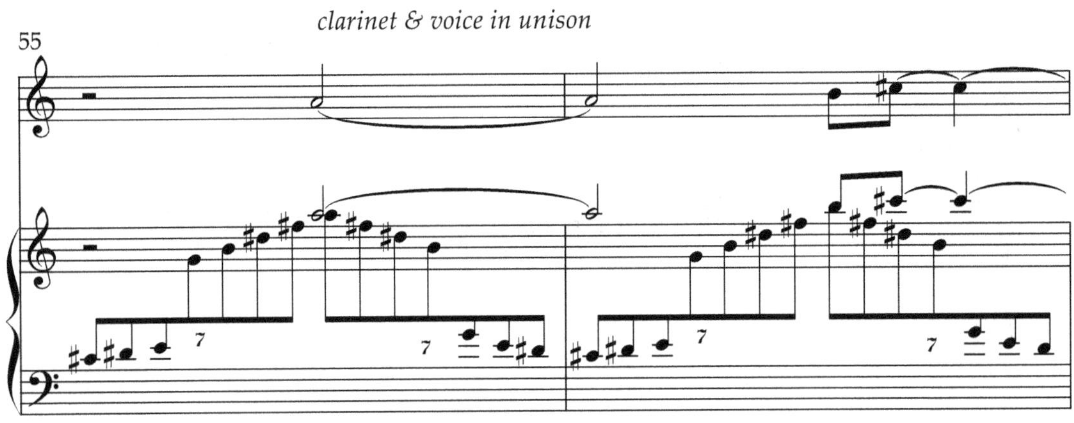
clarinet & voice in unison
55

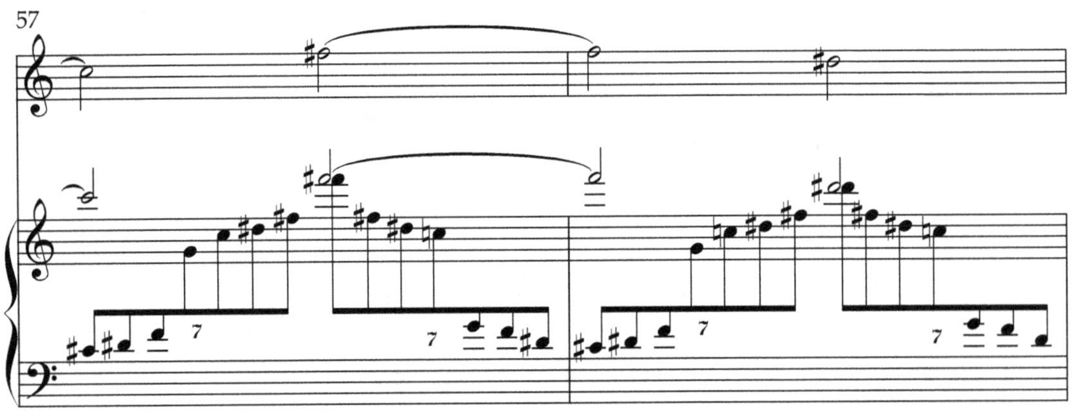
57

59
3
3
7
7
7
7
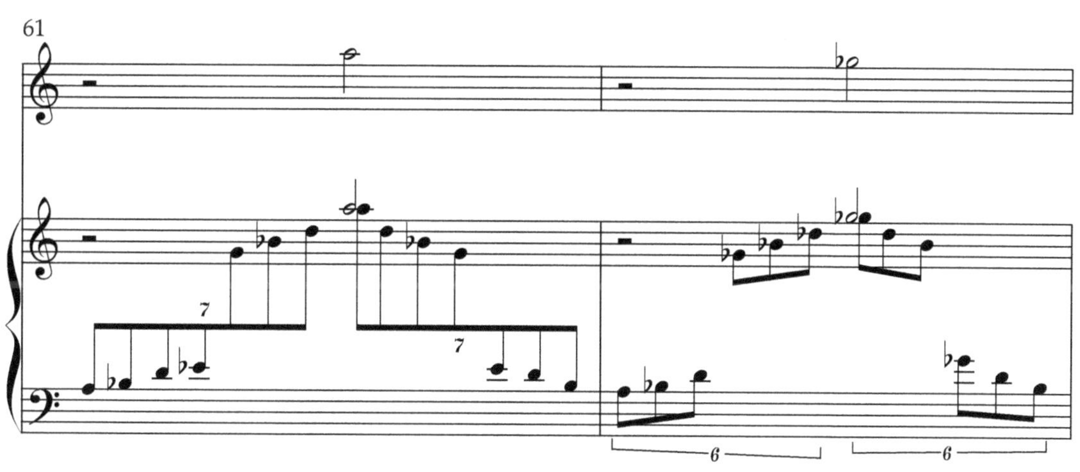
61
7
7
6
6
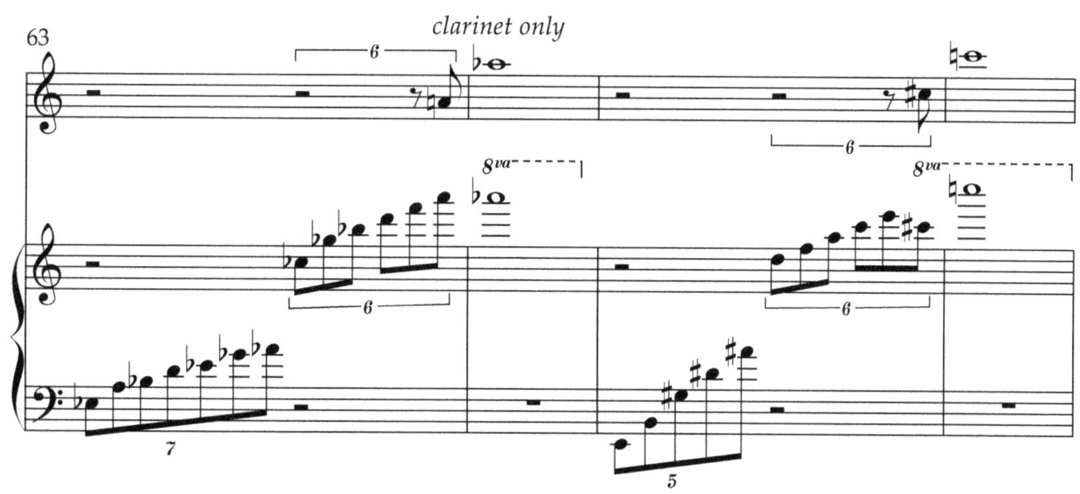
63
clarinet only
6
6
8va
8va
6
6
7
5

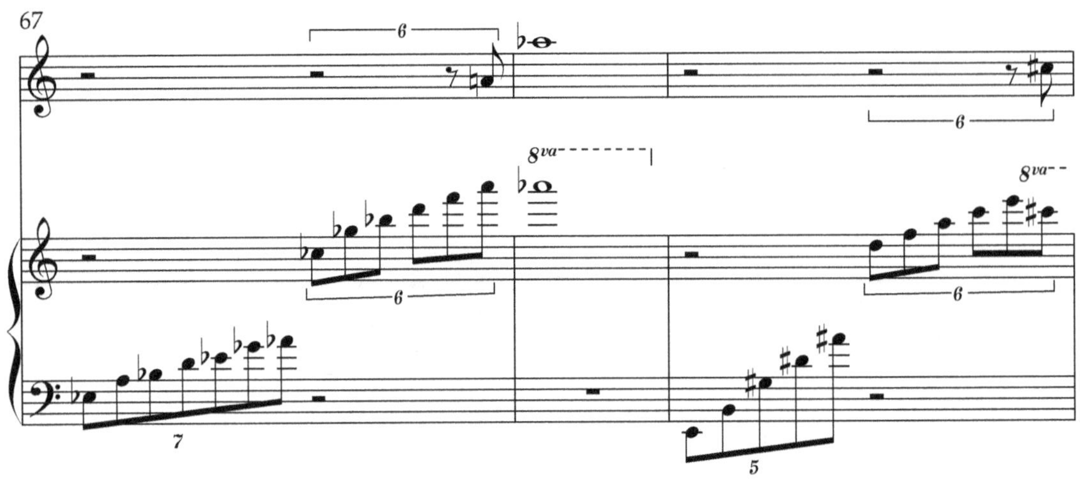
67
8va
6
7
5

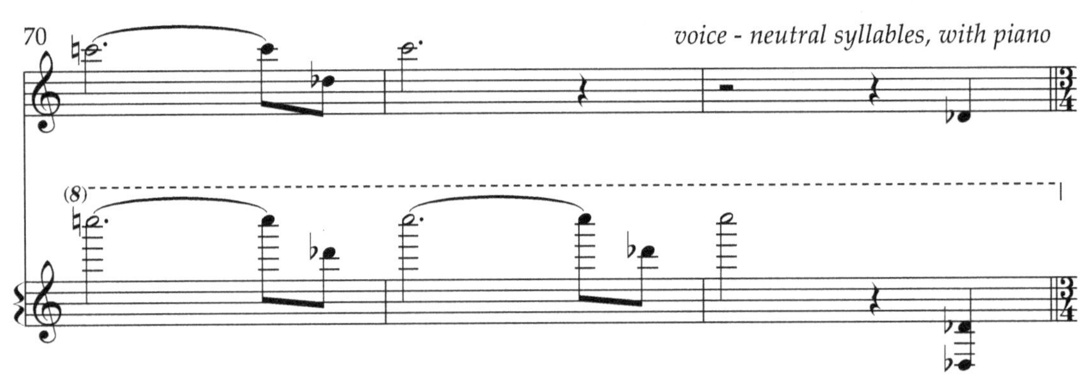
70
voice - neutral syllables, with piano
(8)

73
"Reincarnation"
mf
with pedal

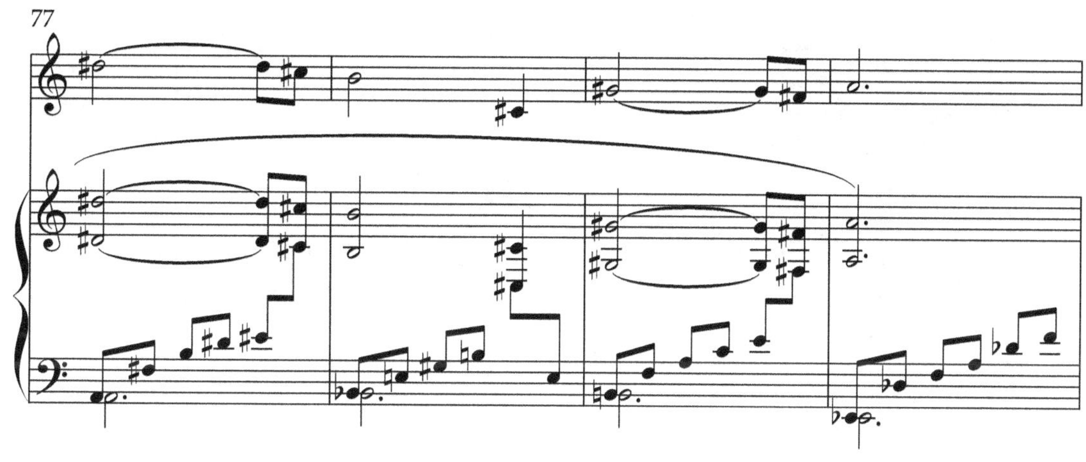
77

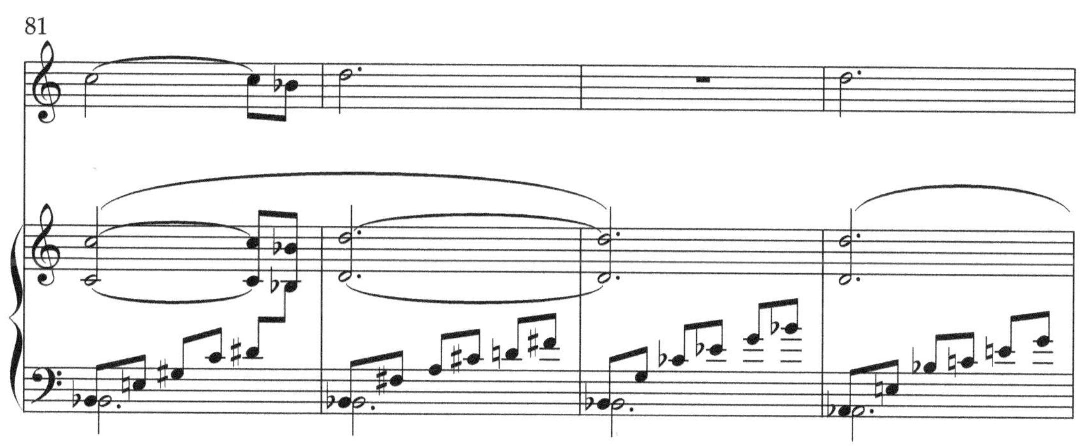
81

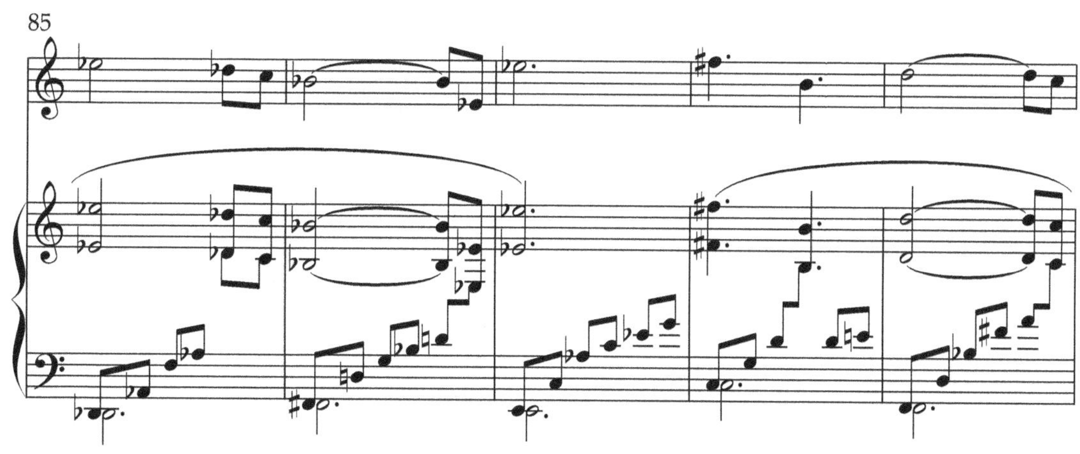
85

90
95
101

105
cresc.

109
cresc. molto

112

115
f
ff
119
decresc.
123
pp

127
slight ritard
(slowly clear pedal)
(pedal cleared)
133
(texture goes to just vocal melody)
Dmaj7
F♯m
Bm
Dmaj7
139
F+
A/C♯
Bmaj7(♯11)/D♯
B♭maj7/D
F/E
145
F♯maj7
F
rit.

Drinking Song

Jeremy Siskind

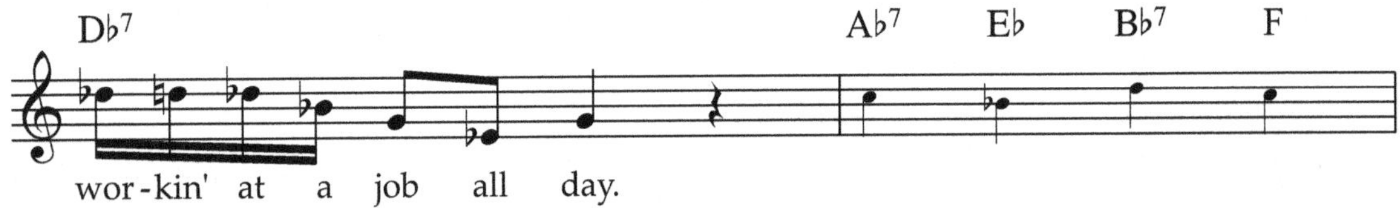

13 Bmaj7
Cmaj7
A♭7
low - life gets a chance at a new life___ when toa - sting

15 D7(♭9)
G7(♯9)
A♭7(♭9)
D♭7
E♭7
G7
"to life,"___ liv - ing fades a way______

17 F♯7
B7
E7(♭9)
A7
A - vi - a - tor gin can make a sad man soar___

19 F♯7
B♭7
E♭maj7
B7
A♭
up a - mong the bar - flies.___ So

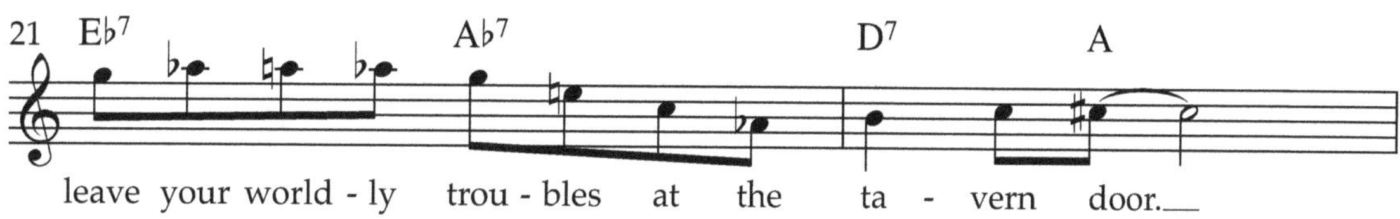
21 E♭7
A♭7
D7
A
leave your world - ly trou - bles at the ta - vern door.___

23 Fm
B7 E7
Am
B♭m
G7
E♭
That hum-drum stuff can't touch you an - y - more. One more pour! fine

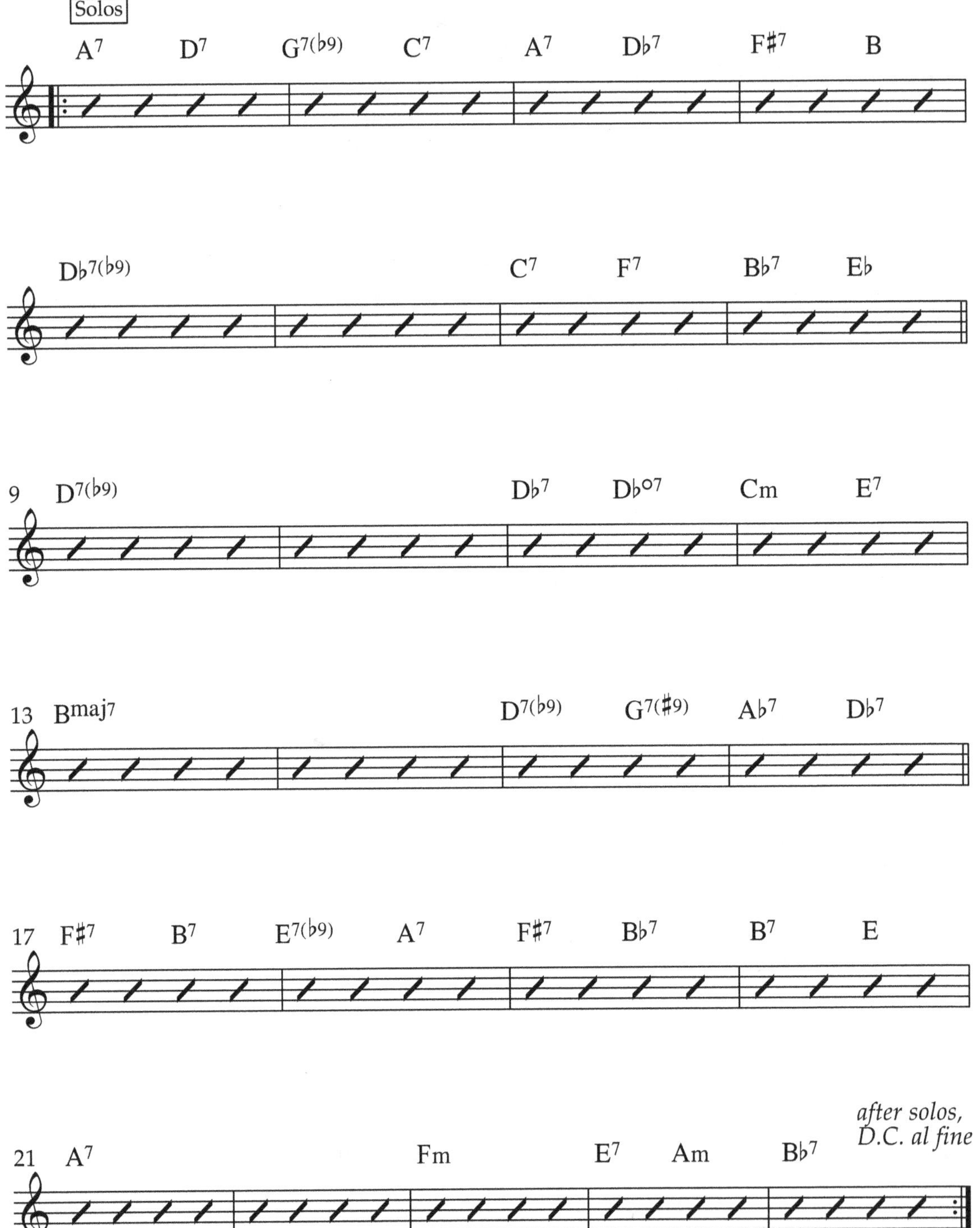
Solos
A7 D7 G7(♭9) C7 A7 D♭7 F♯7 B
D♭7(♭9) C7 F7 B♭7 E♭
9 D7(♭9) D♭7 D♭°7 Cm E7
13 Bmaj7 D7(♭9) G7(♯9) A♭7 D♭7
17 F♯7 B7 E7(♭9) A7 F♯7 B♭7 B7 E
21 A7 Fm E7 Am B♭7
after solos,
D.C. al fine

Serotiny

Slow Tango-Waltz ♩=96

Jeremy Siskind

23 Dm/F B7/F♯ E♭/G
27 Gm/D E♭m Cm
31 A♭m(maj7) Cm/G A♭maj7 G7(♭9)
Voice Enters
35 Cm6/9
Bless this land, this land that burns it - self to
39 Gm/D E♭m
dust each year. the smo - king sea at - tends by
43 E°7 Bm/F♯ G♯ø7
can - dle light, as wood - ed worlds ig - nite.
47 B♭7(♭9) E♭m
The flames pro - claim the gos - pel, the wind, like an a -

50
Em6
F#7alt.
4
pos - tle, sends ash mis - ting down like des - ert

53
Bm
Am6
Em9
rain. Re - lease your seeds.

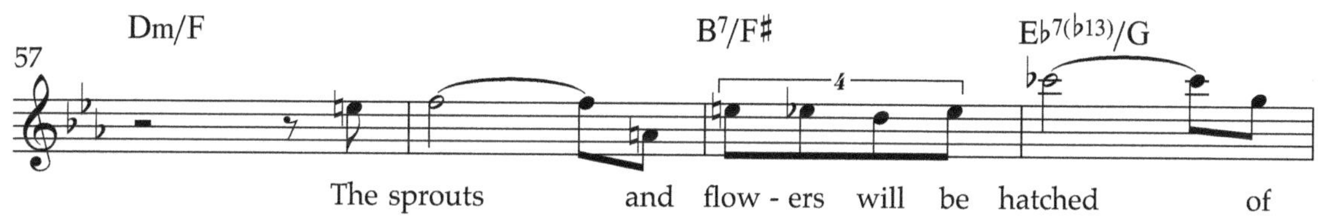
57
Dm/F
B7/F#
Eb7(b13)/G
4
The sprouts and flow - ers will be hatched of

61
Gm/D
Ebm
Cm
Gm
heat. and let the red moon shed tears

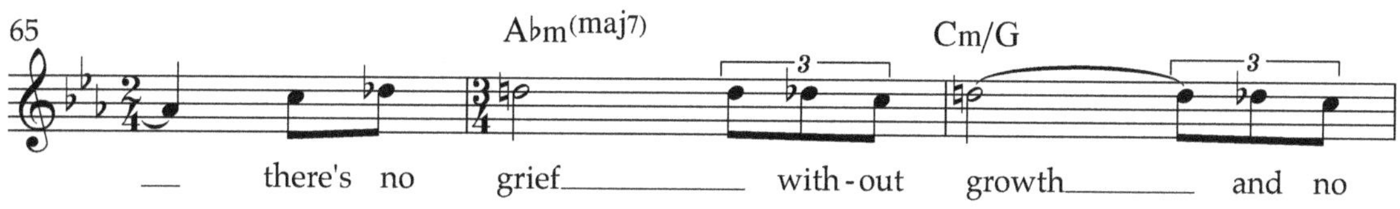
65
Abm(maj7)
Cm/G
3
3
there's no grief with-out growth and no

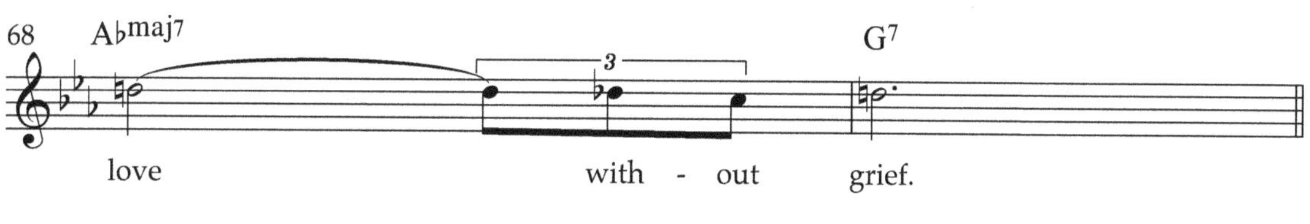
68
Abmaj7
G7
3
love with - out grief.

Solos Over Vamp
70
Abmaj7
G7

I'd Break Quarantine for You

Kneel

Jeremy Siskind

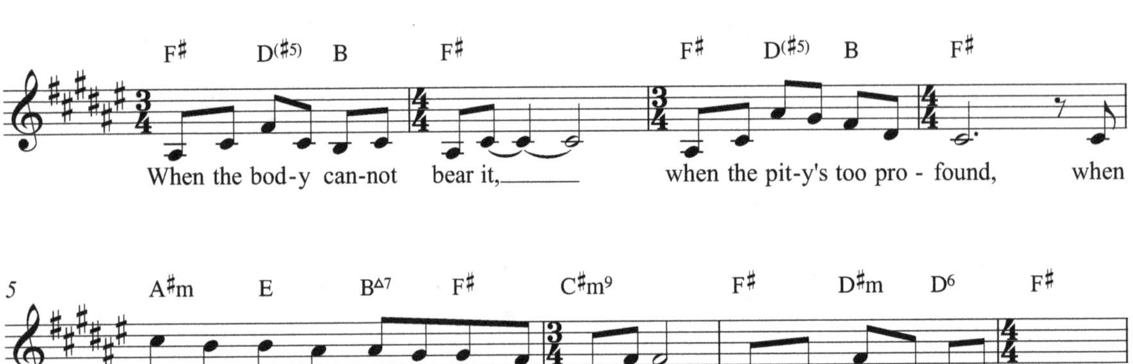

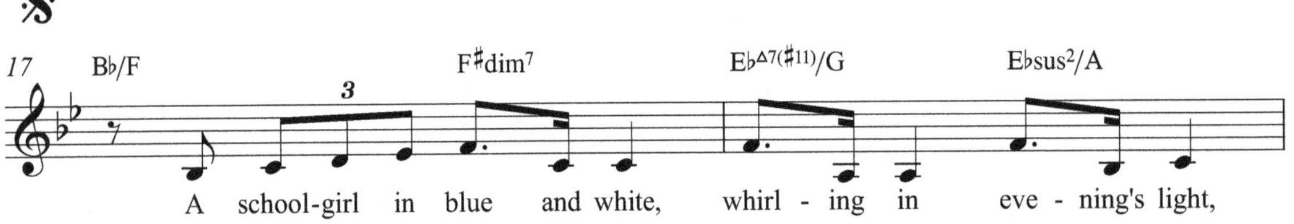

After melody, free improvisation.
Then D.S. al fine.

So, I Went to New York City to Be Born Again

Jeremy Siskind

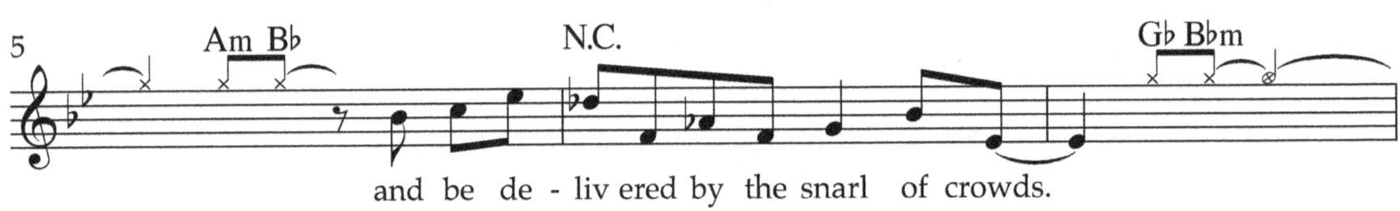

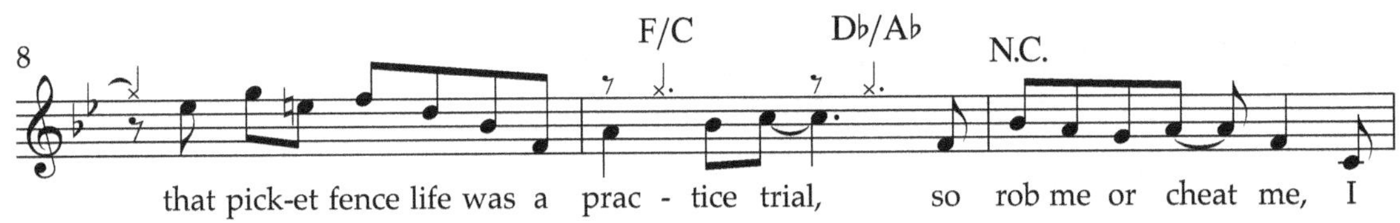

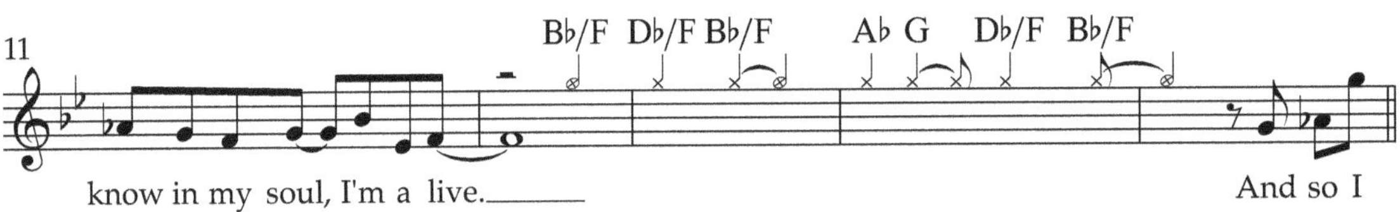

21
a - ve - nue___ and great ev - 'ry sun - rise with a new - born's smile.

23
Am Cm
N.C.
F/G
Star - light a-bove me whis-pered, "You're a - live."_

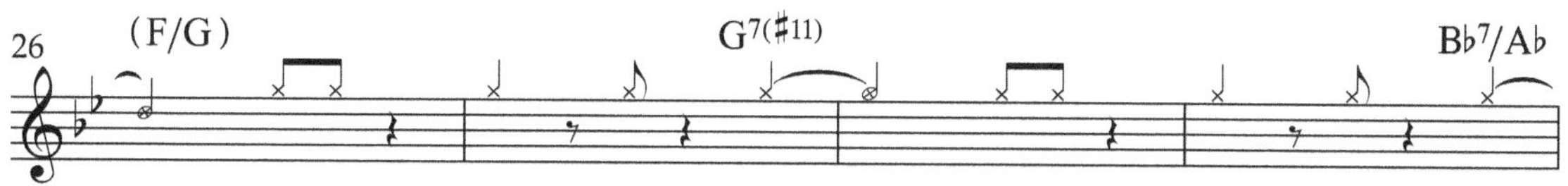
26
(F/G)
G7(♯11)
B♭7/A♭

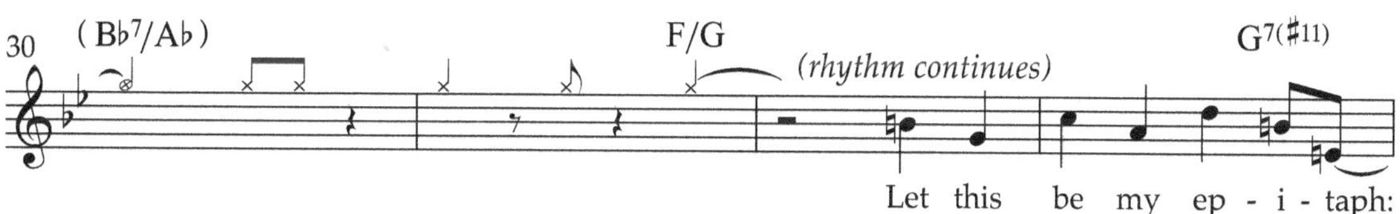
30
(B♭7/A♭)
F/G
(rhythm continues)
G7(♯11)
Let this be my ep - i - taph:

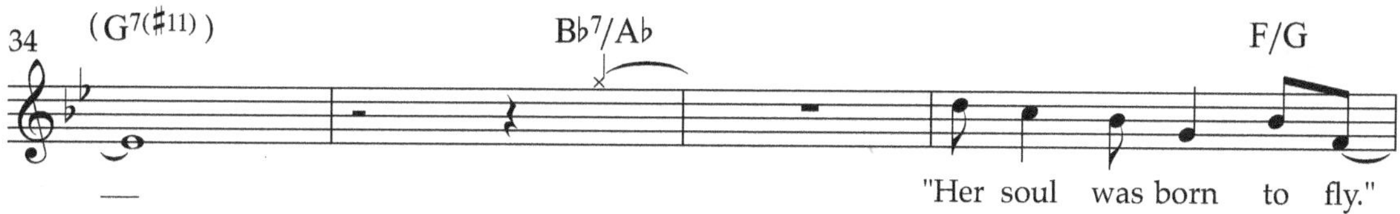
34
(G7(♯11))
B♭7/A♭
F/G
"Her soul was born to fly."

38
(F/G)
G7alt.
B♭7/A♭
Let the small town cri - tics laugh.

42
(B♭7/A♭)
But I ain't a-fraid of I'm not a-fraid of,

46 A♭7(sus4)
I'm not a - fraid of o - pen skies. And so I
50 N.C.
E
E♭ B
D B♭
went to New York Ci-ty to be born a - gain
Solos - Use This Form Until Cue
55 B♭(sus4)
59 B♭(sus4)
63 G(sus4)
67 G(sus4)
71 Emaj7(♯11)
75 Fmaj7(♯11)
A♭7(sus4)
E♭maj7(♯11)
G♭7(sus4)
79 D♭maj7(♯11)
E7(sus4)
Bmaj7(♯11)

Solo On This Form After Cue
82
B♭(sus4)
86
G(sus4)
Continue on Cue
90
Emaj7(♯11)
D♭maj7(♯11)
After Cue
94
B♭maj7
D♭7(sus4)
Fmaj7
A♭7(sus4)
B♭maj7
D♭7(sus4)
F♯m7
Gmaj7(♯11)
98
Bm7
Emaj7(♯11)
Fmaj7
A♭7(sus4)
E♭m7
G♭7(sus4)
D♭maj7(♯11)
101
105
And so I
109
N.C.
G
Am
B♭
G
went to New York Ci - ty to be come brand new.

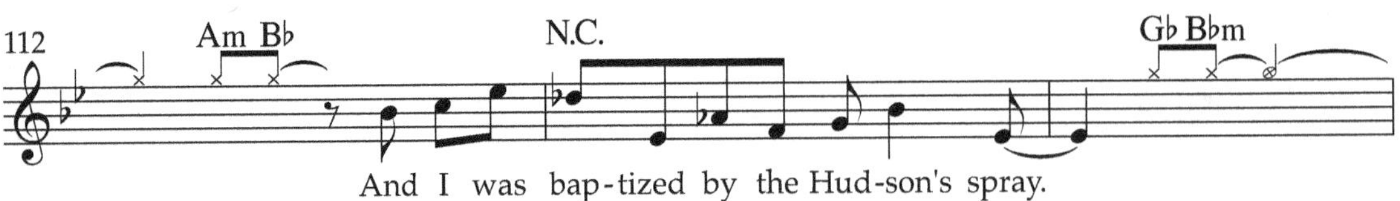
112
Am B♭
N.C.
G♭ B♭m
And I was bap-tized by the Hud-son's spray.

115
F/C
D♭/A♭
My soul a - woke to hear a ven - dor's cry. His

117
N.C.
F/G
voice was like mu - sic, the mel - o - dy said, "you're a - live"

119
F/G
(rhythm continues)
G7(♯11)
B♭7/A♭
Fill my soul with en er gy.

125
(B♭7/A♭)
F/G
G7alt.
Make me a ne -on sign. When the crowds re mem ber me

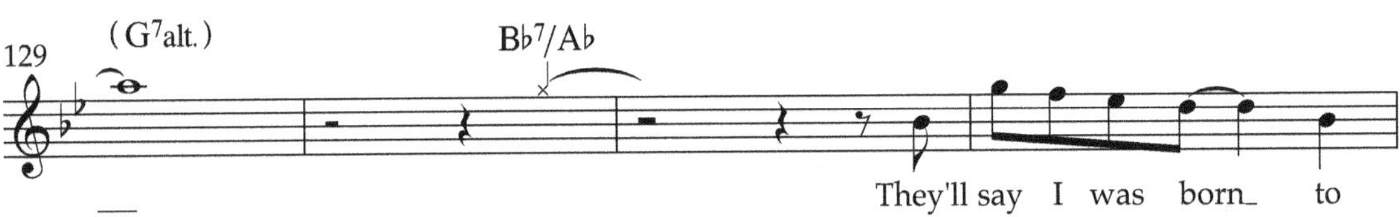
129
(G7alt.)
B♭7/A♭
They'll say I was born_ to

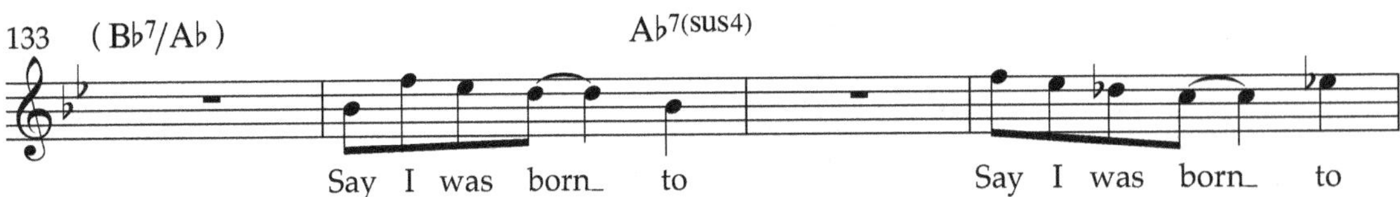
133
(B♭7/A♭)
A♭7(sus4)
Say I was born_ to Say I was born_ to

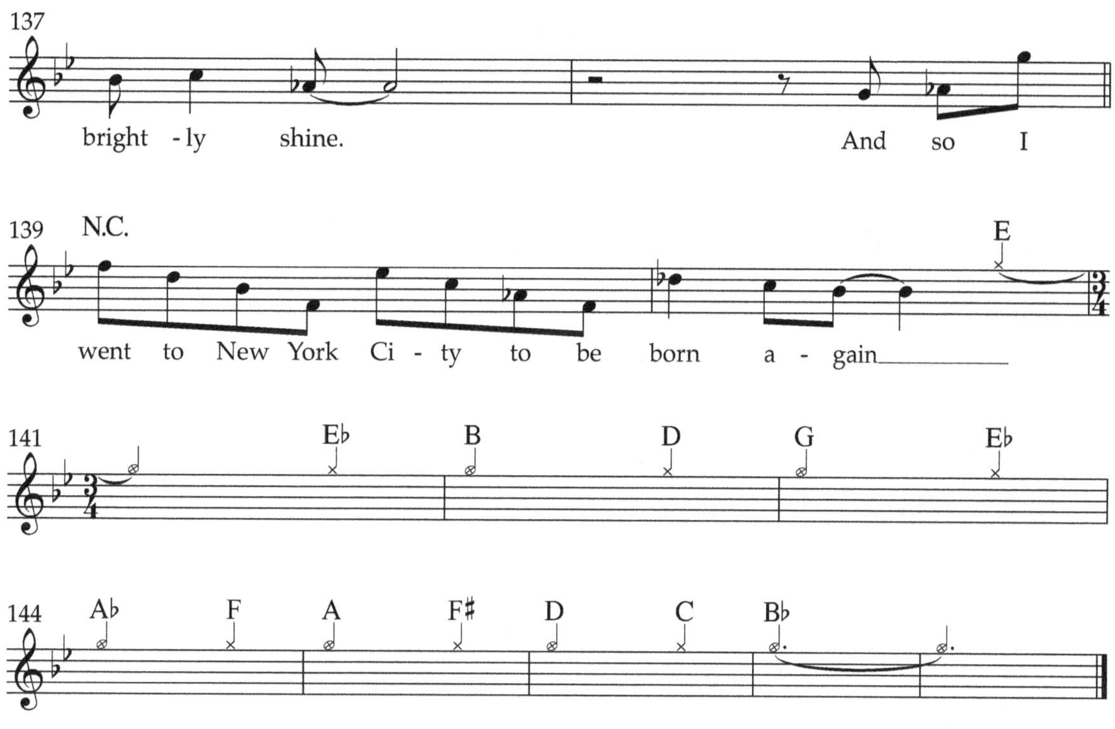
137
bright - ly shine.
And so I
139 N.C.
E
went to New York Ci - ty to be born a - gain
141
E♭
B
D
G
E♭
144 A♭
F
A
F♯
D
C
B♭

New

Jeremy Siskind

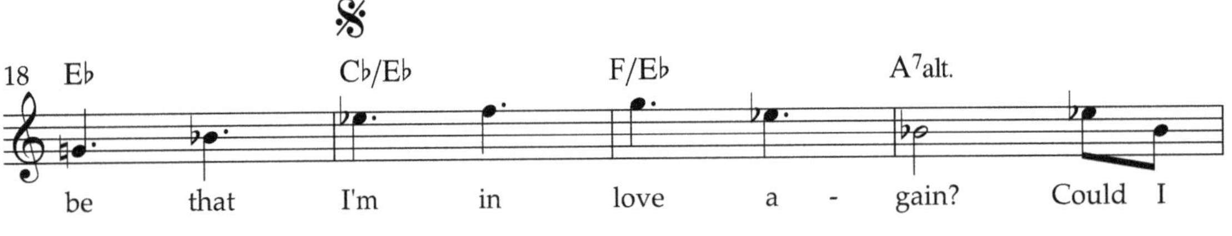

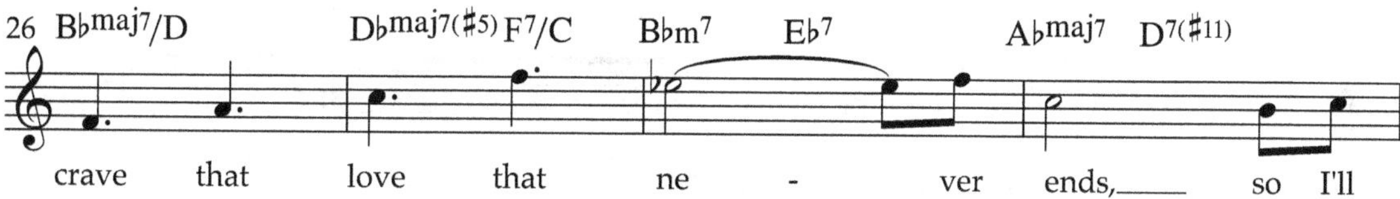
26 B♭maj7/D
D♭maj7(♯5) F7/C
B♭m7
E♭7
A♭maj7
D7(♯11)
crave that love that ne - ver ends, so I'll

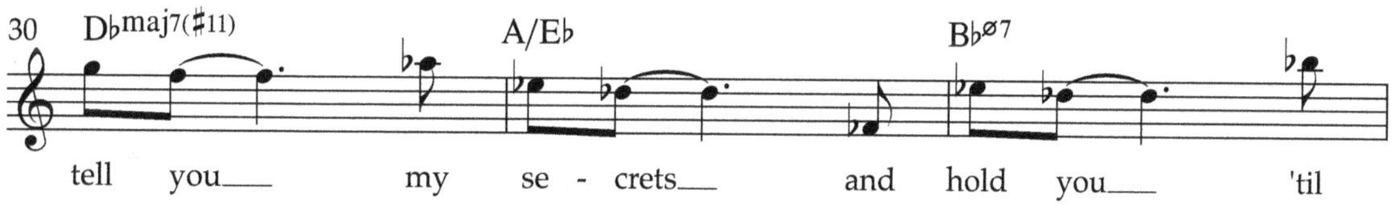
30 D♭maj7(♯11)
A/E♭
B♭ø7
tell you my se - crets and hold you 'til

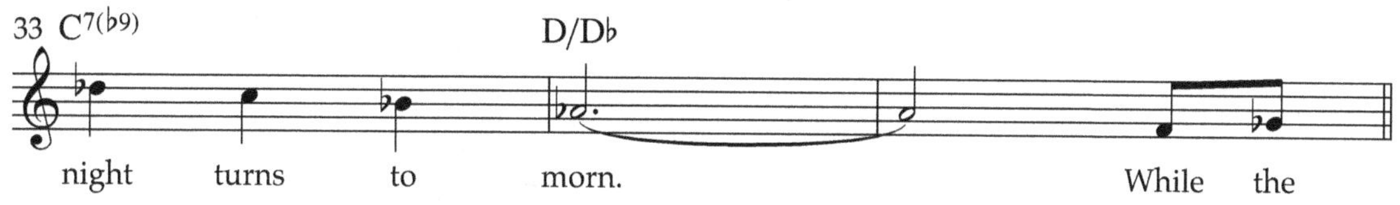
33 C7(♭9)
D/D♭
night turns to morn. While the

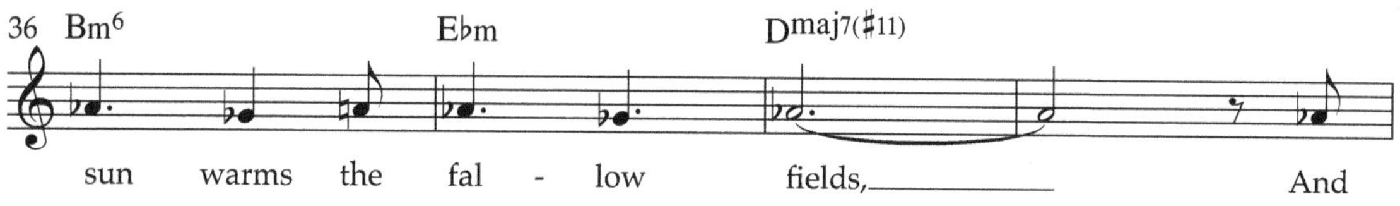
36 Bm6
E♭m
Dmaj7(♯11)
sun warms the fal - low fields, And

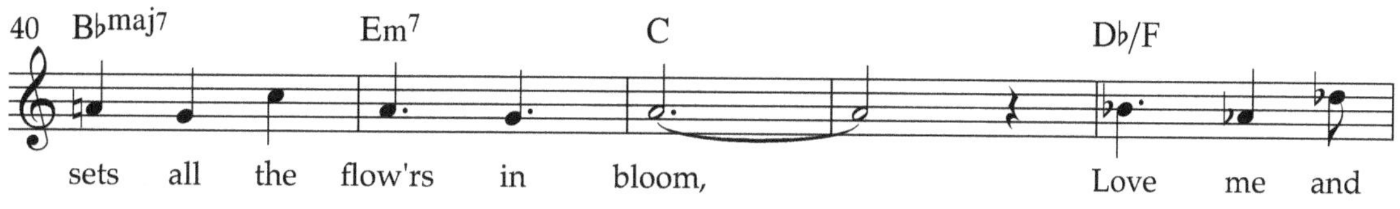
40 B♭maj7
Em7
C
D♭/F
sets all the flow'rs in bloom, Love me and

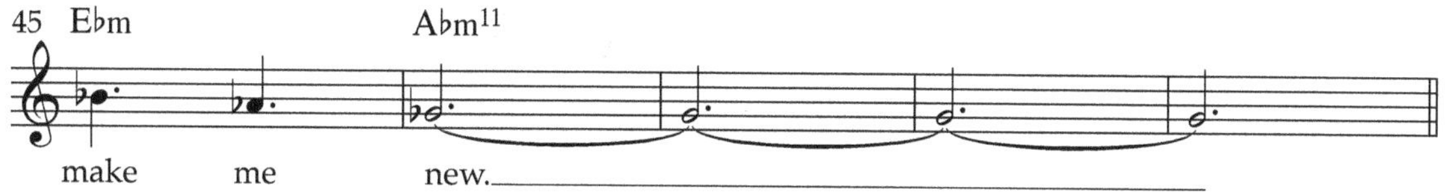
45 E♭m
A♭m11
make me new.

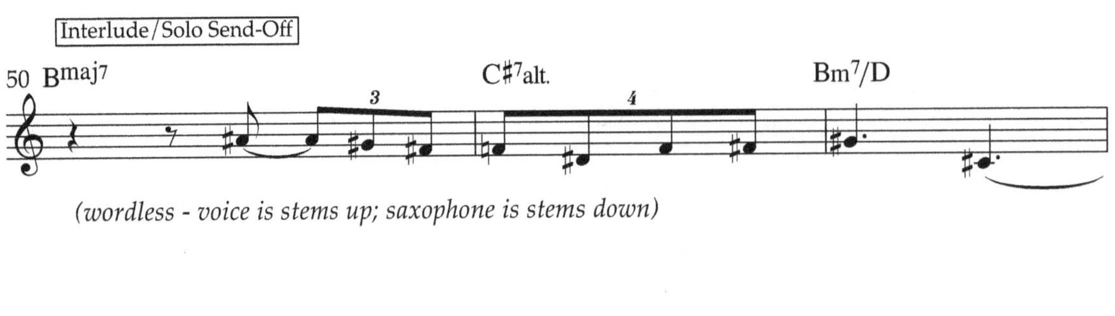

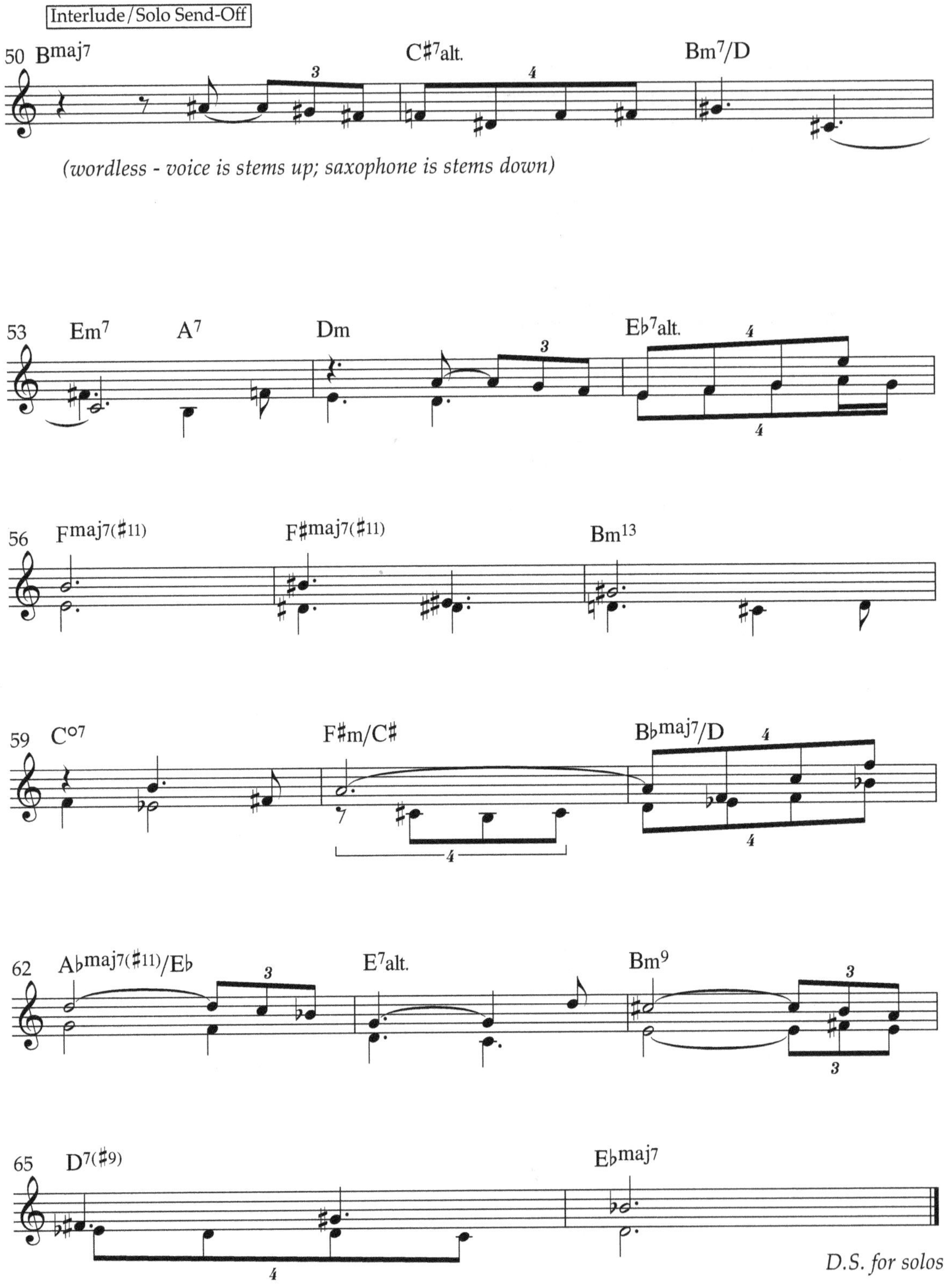

Interlude/Solo Send-Off
50 Bmaj7
C♯7alt.
Bm7/D
(wordless - voice is stems up; saxophone is stems down)
53 Em7
A7
Dm
E♭7alt.
56 Fmaj7(♯11)
F♯maj7(♯11)
Bm13
59 C°7
F♯m/C♯
B♭maj7/D
62 A♭maj7(♯11)/E♭
E7alt.
Bm9
65 D7(♯9)
E♭maj7
D.S. for solos

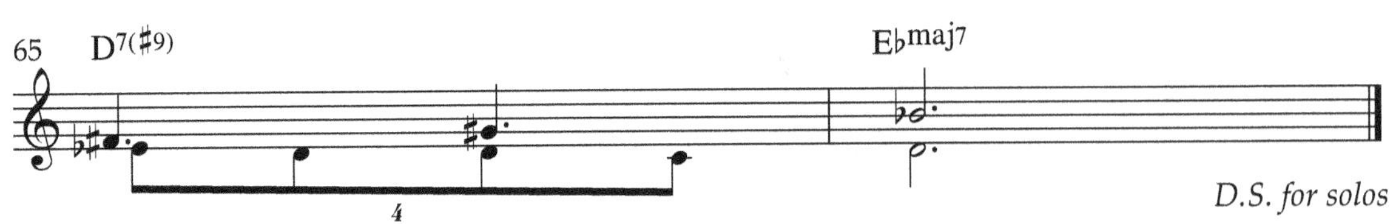

We Will Not Go Back to Normal

Jeremy Siskind

13
Voice
Dream of love, of re - a - wak - e - ning, We've seen the
Pno.
B. Cl.
17
Voice
hoard-ing, ha - ting, suff- 'ring, ra - ging, nor - ma-lized greed,
Pno.
B. Cl.
21
Voice
Friends, let us seek new ways to be.
Pno.
3
B. Cl.

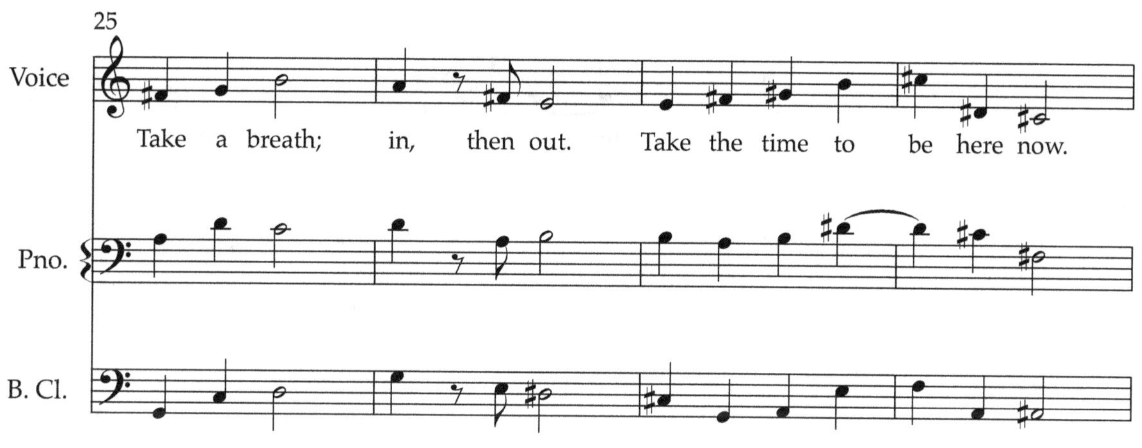
25
Voice
Take a breath; in, then out. Take the time to be here now.
Pno.
B. Cl.

29
Voice
Now we're called to heal our hurt, so let's make the hea - ling
Pno.
B. Cl.

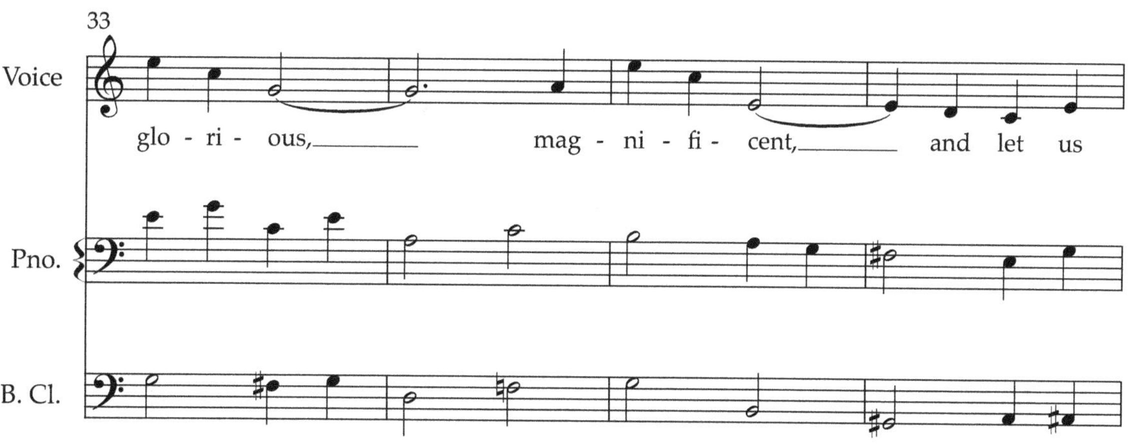
33
Voice
glo - ri - ous, mag - ni - fi - cent, and let us
Pno.
B. Cl.

37
Voice
not re- turn,
not re-wind,
not re - peat,
re - vert, reach
Pno.
B. Cl.
41
Voice
out your hand,
take hold of mine.
Pno.
3
3
3
B. Cl.
45
Voice
un - der- stand, to geth - er, we can make this right.
Pno.
B. Cl.

49
Voice
Let this be our prayer, help us love oth - ers, Lord. ah
Pno.
B. Cl.
53
Voice
Let this be our prayer, help us to love our-selves too.
Pno.
B. Cl.
56
Voice
ah let's make it new.
Pno.
B. Cl.

59
Pno.
B. Cl.
63
Pno.
B. Cl.
67
Pno.
B. Cl.
71
Pno.
B. Cl.
75
Pno.
3
3
B. Cl.
3

79
(wordless)
Voice
Pno.
B. Cl.
(melody)

83
Voice
Pno.
B. Cl.

87
Voice
Pno.
B. Cl.

91
Voice
Pno.
B. Cl.

95
Voice
Take my hand, hold it tight, take a breath, close your eyes.
Pno.
B. Cl.

99
Voice
Take the time to free your mind and dream.
Pno.
B. Cl.

103
Voice
Dream a dream of what the spring could be.
Pno.
3
B. Cl.

107
Voice
3
Let this be our prayer, help us love oth - ers, Lord. ah
Pno.
3
B. Cl.
3

111
Voice
3
3
Let this be our prayer, help us to love our-selves too.
Pno.
3
3
B. Cl.
3

114
Voice
ah
Help us, Lord,
to make it new.
Pno.
B. Cl.

Disc 2 Leadsheets and Scores

Growing Pains

Jeremy Siskind

29
D♯°7
D♯ø7
D♯7(♭5)
G/D
B7(♯9)

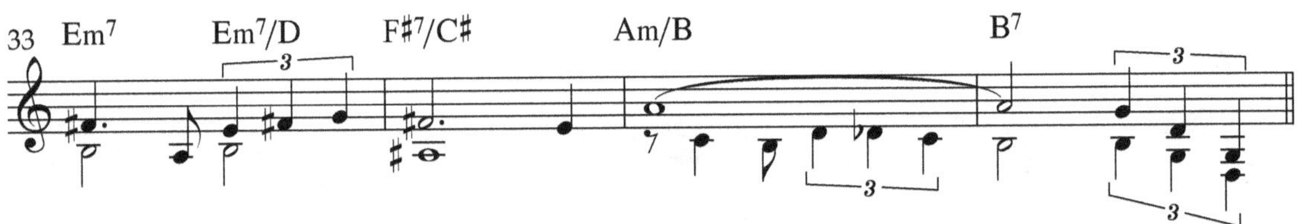
33
Em7
Em7/D
F♯7/C♯
Am/B
B7
3
3
3

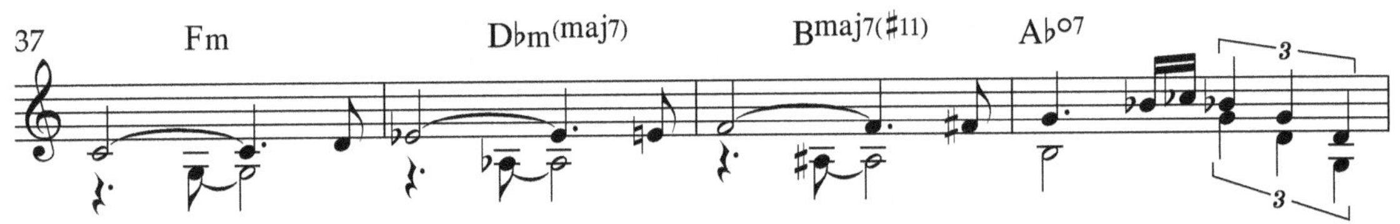
37
Fm
D♭m(maj7)
Bmaj7(♯11)
A♭°7
3
3

41
D♭maj7
D/B♭
B/G
Cmaj7(♯11)
3
3

45
D♭
Gmaj7(♯11)
E♭m7(♭6)
B♭/D

49
Emaj7(♯11)
C7alt.
Bmaj7

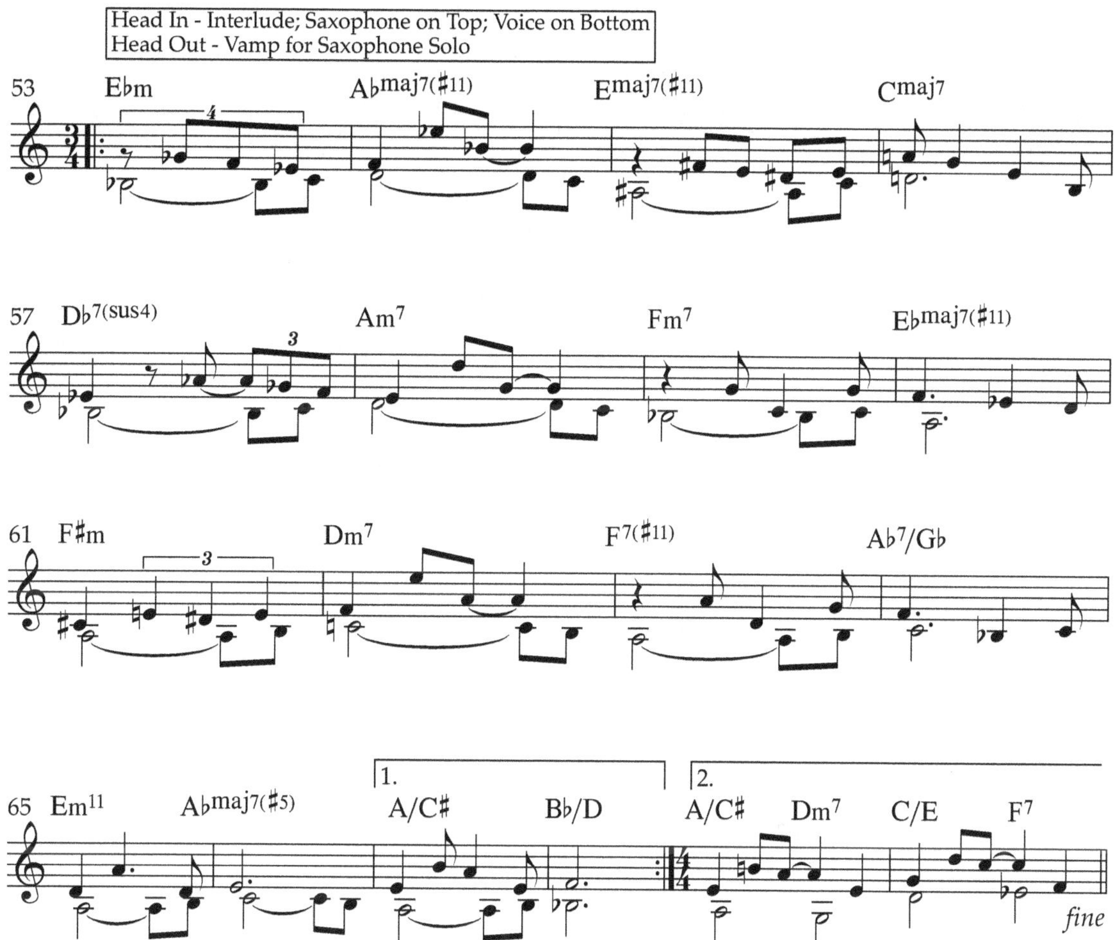
Head In - Interlude; Saxophone on Top; Voice on Bottom
Head Out - Vamp for Saxophone Solo
53
E♭m
A♭maj7(♯11)
Emaj7(♯11)
Cmaj7
57
D♭7(sus4)
Am7
Fm7
E♭maj7(♯11)
61
F♯m
Dm7
F7(♯11)
A♭7/G♭
65
Em11
A♭maj7(♯5)
1.
A/C♯
B♭/D
2.
A/C♯
Dm7
C/E
F7
fine

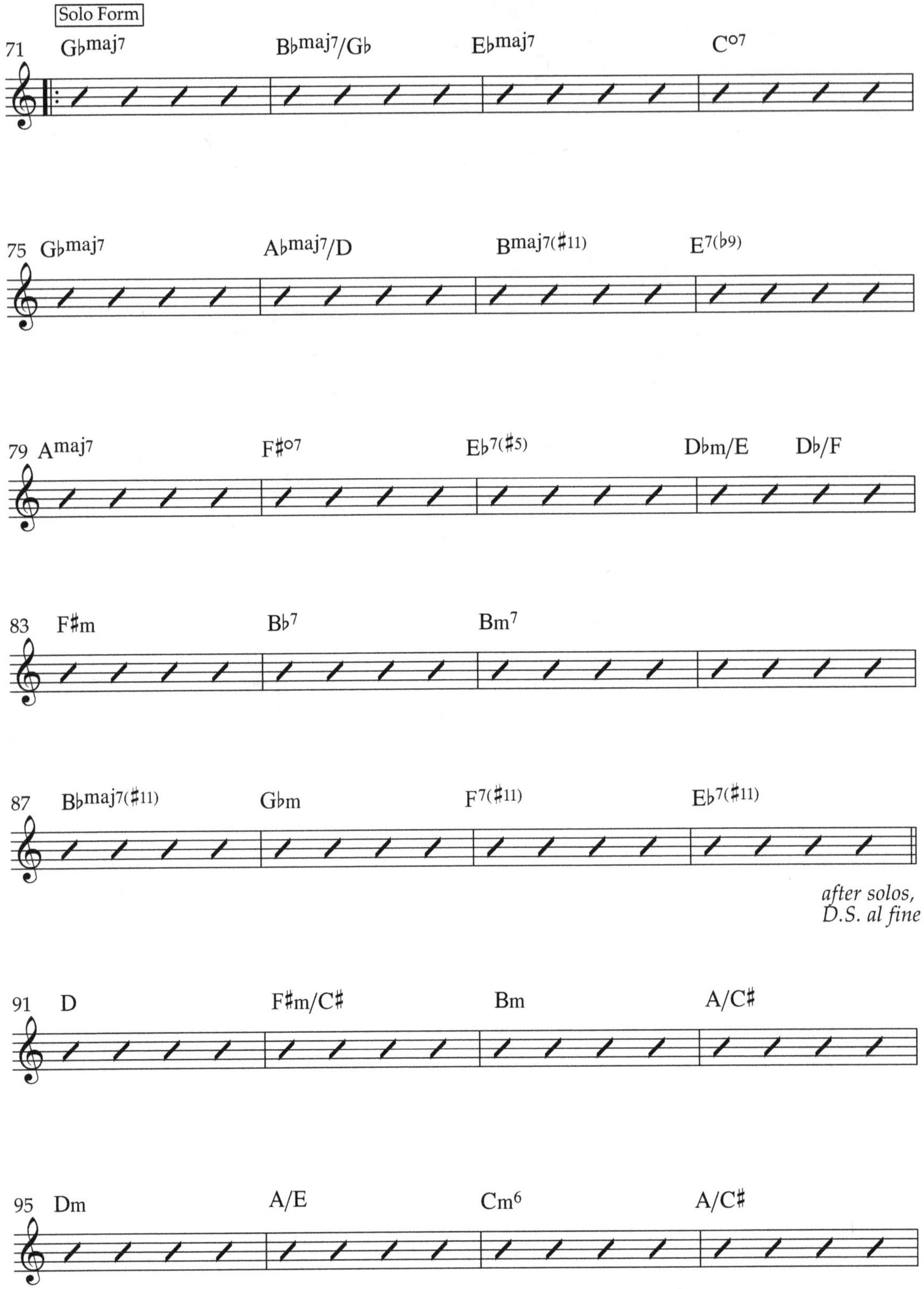

Solo Form

71 G♭maj7 | B♭maj7/G♭ | E♭maj7 | C°7

75 G♭maj7 | A♭maj7/D | Bmaj7(♯11) | E7(♭9)

79 Amaj7 | F♯°7 | E♭7(♯5) | D♭m/E D♭/F

83 F♯m | B♭7 | Bm7 |

87 B♭maj7(♯11) | G♭m | F7(♯11) | E♭7(♯11)

after solos, D.S. al fine

91 D | F♯m/C♯ | Bm | A/C♯

95 Dm | A/E | Cm6 | A/C♯

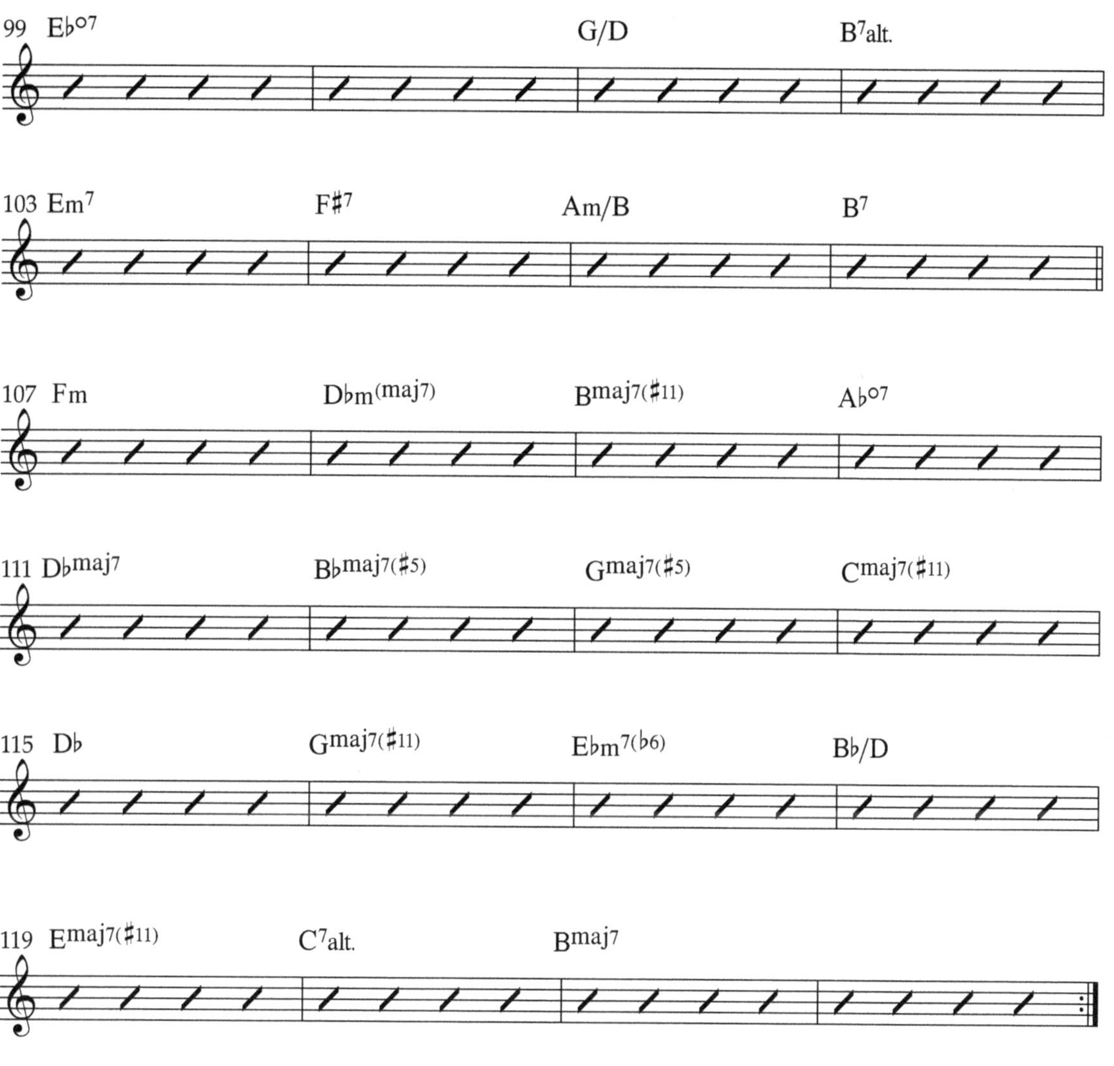
99 E♭°7 G/D B7alt.
103 Em7 F♯7 Am/B B7
107 Fm D♭m(maj7) Bmaj7(♯11) A♭°7
111 D♭maj7 B♭maj7(♯5) Gmaj7(♯5) Cmaj7(♯11)
115 D♭ Gmaj7(♯11) E♭m7(♭6) B♭/D
119 Emaj7(♯11) C7alt. Bmaj7

I'd Break Quarantine for You

Long Beach, In Fog

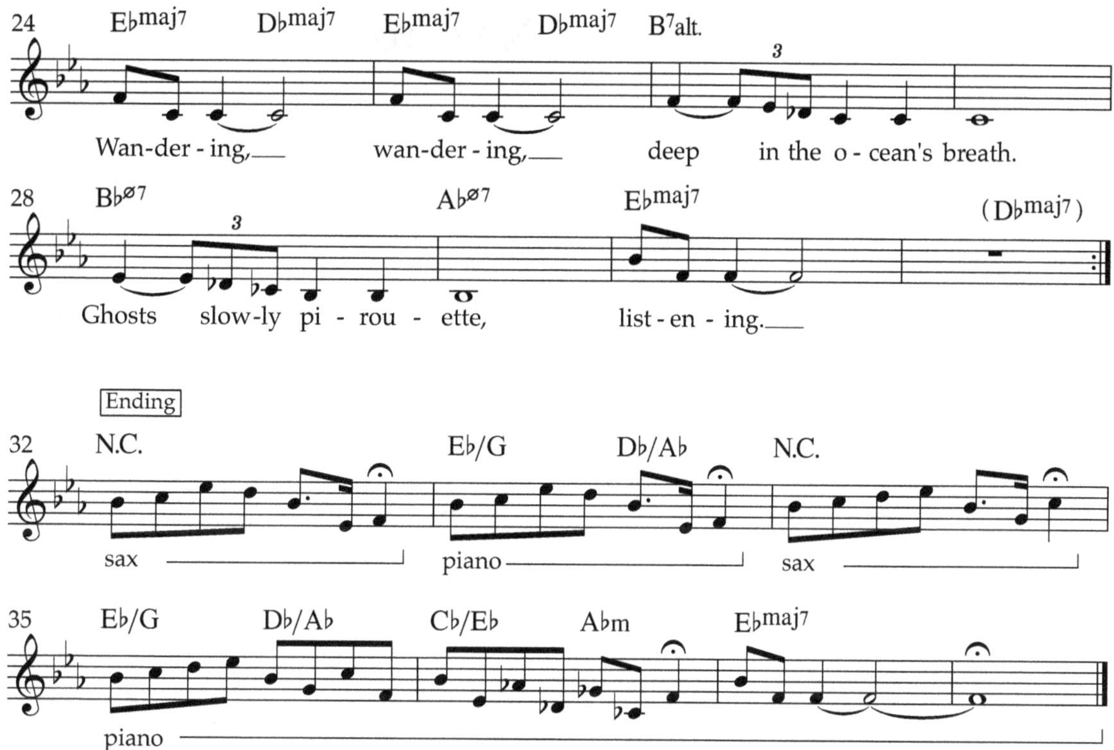
24
E♭maj7 D♭maj7 E♭maj7 D♭maj7 B7alt.
3
Wan-der - ing, wan-der - ing, deep in the o - cean's breath.
28
B♭ø7 A♭ø7 E♭maj7 (D♭maj7)
3
Ghosts slow-ly pi - rou - ette, list - en - ing.
Ending
32
N.C. E♭/G D♭/A♭ N.C.
sax piano sax
35
E♭/G D♭/A♭ C♭/E♭ A♭m E♭maj7
piano

New Year, New You

Jeremy Siskind

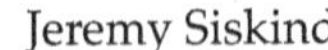

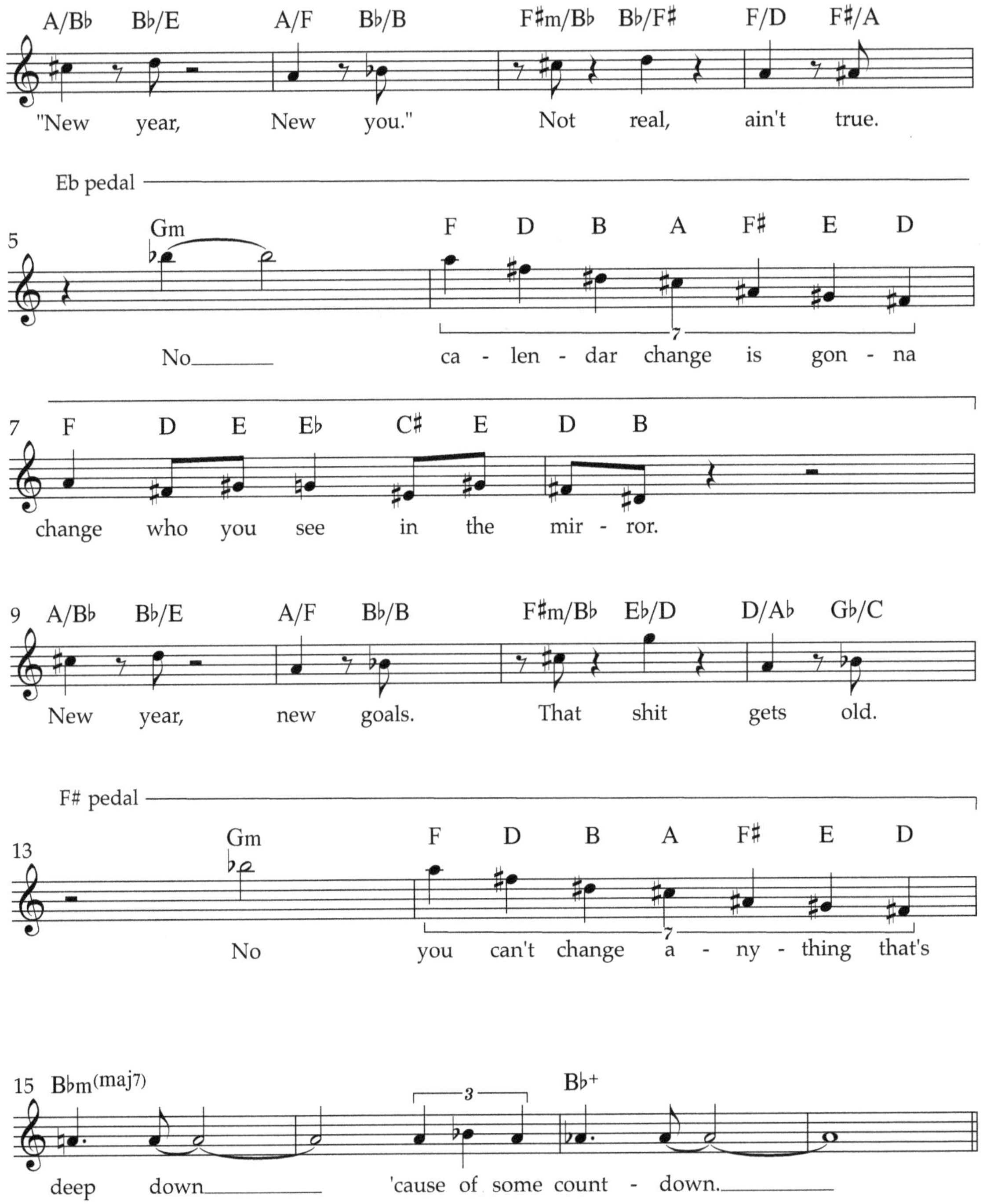
A/B♭ B♭/E A/F B♭/B F♯m/B♭ B♭/F♯ F/D F♯/A
"New year, New you." Not real, ain't true.
Eb pedal
5
Gm
F D B A F♯ E D
7
No ca - len - dar change is gon - na
7 F D E E♭ C♯ E D B
change who you see in the mir - ror.
9 A/B♭ B♭/E A/F B♭/B F♯m/B♭ E♭/D D/A♭ G♭/C
New year, new goals. That shit gets old.
F# pedal
13
Gm
F D B A F♯ E D
7
No you can't change a - ny - thing that's
15 B♭m(maj7)
3
B♭+
deep down 'cause of some count - down.

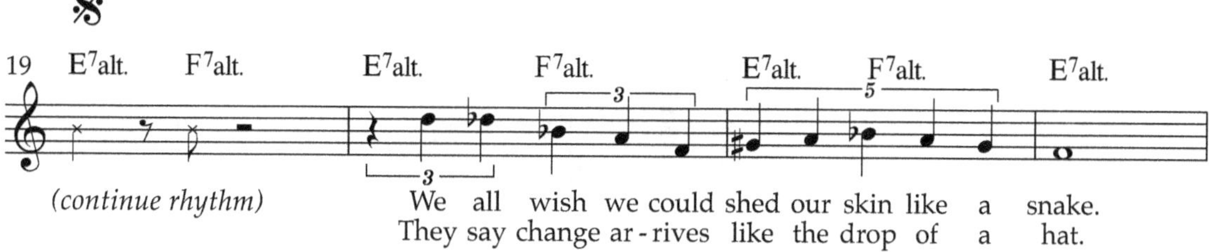
19
E7alt.
F7alt.
E7alt.
F7alt.
E7alt.
F7alt.
E7alt.
(continue rhythm)
We all wish we could shed our skin like a snake.
They say change ar-rives like the drop of a hat.

23
A7alt.
Bb7alt.
A7alt.
Bb7alt.
A7alt.
Bb7alt.
A7alt. Ab7alt.
Bro-ther it ain't that sim - ple.
Real life ain't so fick - le.

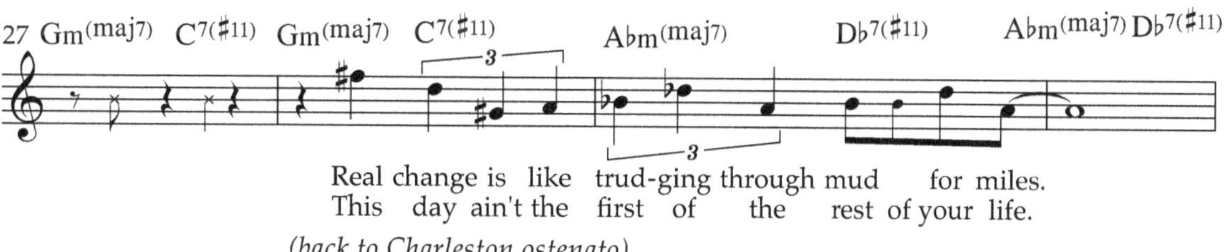
27
Gm(maj7)
C7(#11)
Gm(maj7)
C7(#11)
Abm(maj7)
Db7(#11)
Abm(maj7) Db7(#11)
Real change is like trud-ging through mud for miles.
This day ain't the first of the rest of your life.
(back to Charleston ostenato)

31
F#
C
F#
C
Gb/G
D/Ab
A/Bb
Real change ain't like pop-ping a pim- ple.
It's just one more day in the mid-dle.

Instrumental Unison/Mirror Line
35

37

38 A/B♭ B♭/E A/F B♭/B F♯m/B♭ B♭/F♯ F/D F♯/A
"New year, new you." Not real, ain't true.
42 A/F♯ D♭/B B♭/E E♭/D♭ B♭+/E♭ B/G A/F B♭
New year, be bold. It all makes me feels old.
New year, can't lie. Each year, I still try.
sub. p
fine
Solos
46 A/B♭ B♭/E A/F B♭/B F♯m/B♭ B♭/F♯ F/D F♯/A
50 E♭7
54 A/B♭ B♭/E A/F B♭/B F♯m/B♭ E♭/D D/A♭ G♭/C
58 F♯7 B♭m B♭+7
second time, D.S. al fine
64 E7alt. F7alt. E7alt. F7alt. E7alt. F7alt. E7alt. F7alt. A7alt. B♭7alt.
69 A7alt. B♭7alt. A7alt. B♭7alt, A7alt. A♭7alt. Gm(maj7) C7(♯11) Gm(maj7) C7(♯11)

74 A♭m(maj7) D♭7(♯11) A♭m(maj7) D♭7(♯11) F♯ C F♯ C
78 G♭/G D/A♭ A/B♭
Instrumental Unison / Mirror Line
80
3
3
82
83 A/B♭ B♭/E A/F B♭/B F♯m/B♭ B♭/F♯ F/D F♯/A
87 A/F♯ D♭/B B♭/E E♭/D♭ B♭+/E♭ B/G A/F B♭

I'd Break Quarantine for You

April, the Liar

Jeremy Siskind

24 Am/C B7 A7/C♯
daf - fo - dils are love - ly, don't be
27 Dm A♭7(♯9)/C E/B
fooled, no flow - er brings per - en - ni - al
30 F♯/A♯ Gmaj7(♯11) C♯7 G♭maj7/C
youth. We're all gon-na die. A - pril's a
35 Fm G♭m A♭maj7 Am(maj7)
lie.
39 Fm G♭m A♭maj7 Am(maj7)

Demeter

Jeremy Siskind

25
C5
Dm
Bm
D♭
Bring me dreams of fields and flow'rs. My
29
Fm
C♭
E♭m
B♭m
daugh - ter paints the fields and the flow'rs, but my
33
A/C♯
Am/E
Em
daugh - ter's been sto - len a - way. and the
In Time; Roiling
37
Bm
G5
A5
fields are just dirt, dust, and clay.
fine
First Time: As Written - Unison
Second Time: Repeat for Solos
41
A5
4
4
(no lyrics)
45
4
49
C♯5
3

53
E5

57
Dm7
F♯m

61
C
D♭

65
Fm
C♭
E♭m
B♭m

69
A/C♯
Am/E
Em

Continue After Cue
73
Bm
Gm
A

After Solos, Unison, Out of Time
77
A5
4
4
81
4
85
3
89
D.S. al fine

I'd Break Quarantine for You

Jeremy Siskind

Forgiveness

Jeremy Siskind

13
F
Gm11
B♭/D
C/E
wrote to you last year. and I
15
F
G7(add4)
D7(add4)
F(♯11)
made my a - pol - o - gy. I should have sent it
(notice change)
17
G7(add4)
G(add4)/D
C/E
G7(sus4)
long a - go. You must have felt
19
D7(♯11)
E+
G7(sus4)
D7(♯11)
so a - lone, but you should know when I'm
21
C♯m
F♯(add4)
Amaj7(♯11)
Bm7
F♯m7(♭6)
on the train, I watch the years roll by like end-less hills. 'Though

25
Fmaj7
E+
Dm7
Gm7
C7(sus4)
you and I ___ have trav - eled dif - f'rent tracks, I think a - bout you
29
Begin Solo
D.S. to continue solo
still.
Interlude
33
F
Gm11
B♭/D
C/E
F
G7(add4)
Dm7
E7
37
Fm
Gm11
B♭/D
E+
39
Fm
Cm/G
B♭/D
C/E
41
F
Gm11
B♭/D
C/E
F
G7(add4)
44
D7(sus4)
F(♯11)
G7(add4)
G(add4)/D
C/E
G7(sus4)
47
D7(♯11)
E+
G7(sus4)
D7(♯11)
when I'm

49
C♯m
F♯(add4)
Amaj7(♯11)
Bm7
F♯m7(♭6)
on the train, I watch the years roll by like end-less hills. 'Though
53
Fmaj7
E+
Dm7
Gm7
C7(sus4)
you and I have trav-eled dif-f'rent tracks, I think a-bout you
57
still.
I
61
F
Gm11
B♭/D
C/E
F
G7(add4)
wake to mor-ning sun, and once more re-a-lize you're
64
Dm7
E7
Fm
Gm7
B♭/D
C/E
gone. can you for-give me, my friend?
67
F
Gm11
B♭/D
C/E
F
B♭/D
C/E
vamp and fade

Another Birthday

Jeremy Siskind

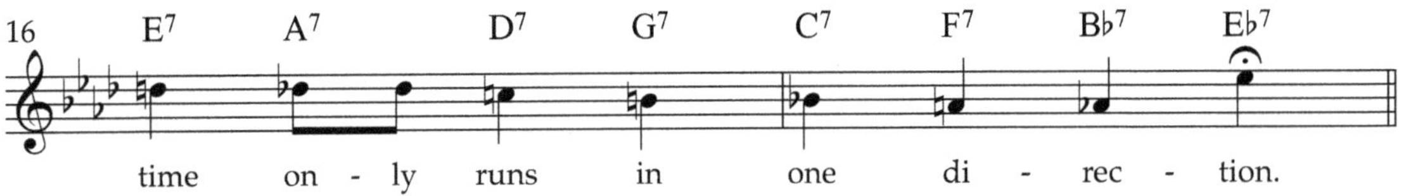

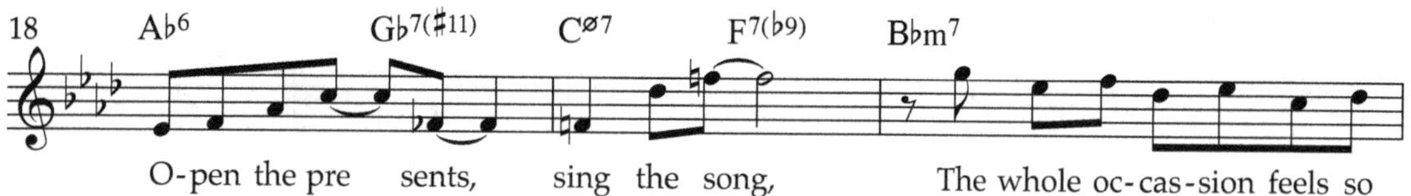
18
A♭6 G♭7(♯11) Cø7 F7(♭9) B♭m7
O-pen the pre sents, sing the song, The whole oc-cas-sion feels so

21
E♭7 E♭m7 B♭7(♯9) E♭m7 A♭7(♭9)
child-ish. Be a good sport and play a - long.

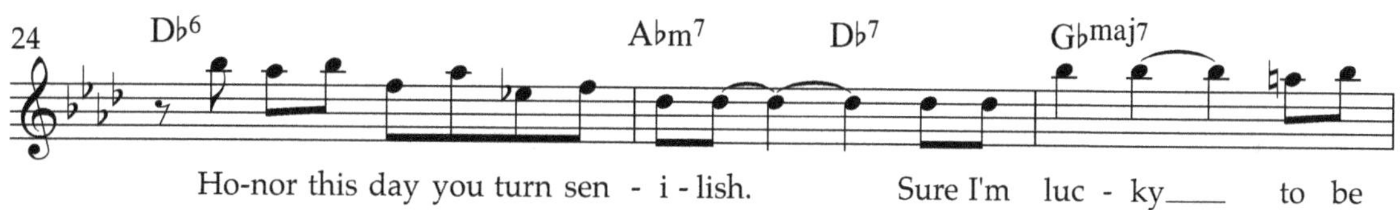
24
D♭6 A♭m7 D♭7 G♭maj7
Ho-nor this day you turn sen - i - lish. Sure I'm luc - ky to be

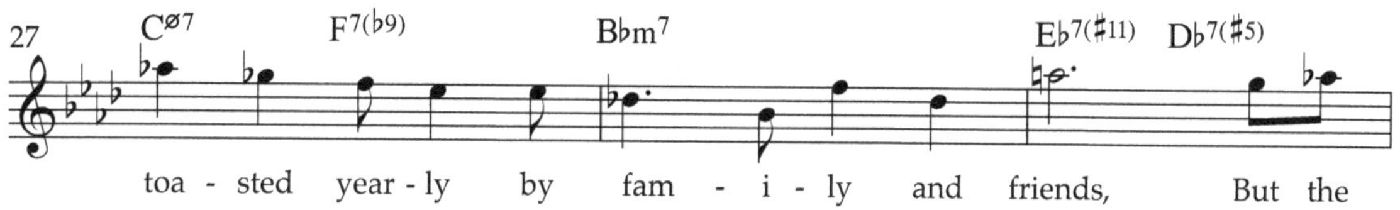
27
Cø7 F7(♭9) B♭m7 E♭7(♯11) D♭7(♯5)
toa - sted year - ly by fam - i - ly and friends, But the

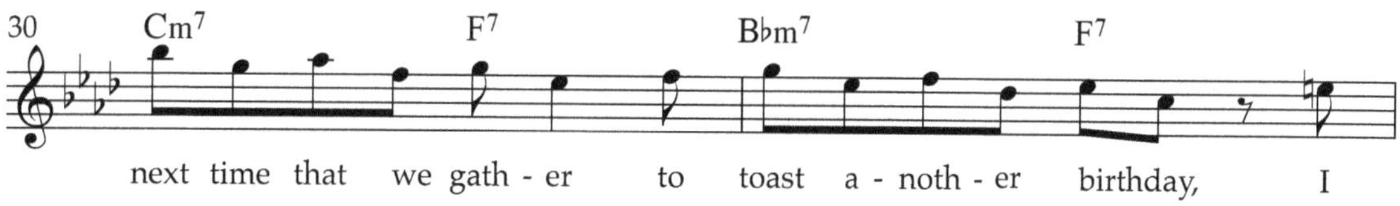
30
Cm7 F7 B♭m7 F7
next time that we gath - er to toast a - noth - er birthday, I

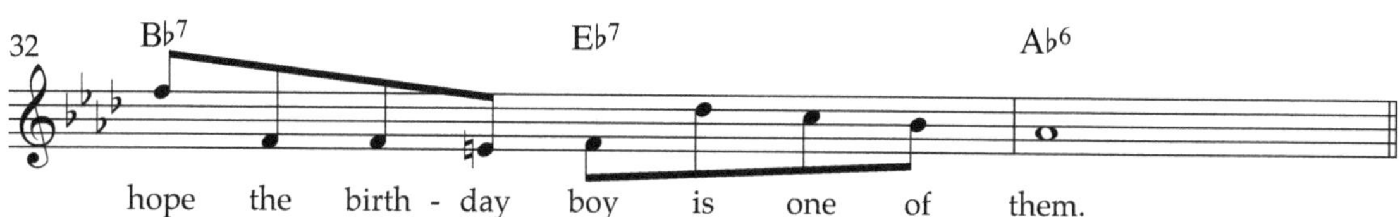
32
B♭7 E♭7 A♭6
hope the birth - day boy is one of them.

34 A♭6 G♭7(♯11) C⌀7 F7(♭9) B♭m7 E♭7(♯11)
38 B♭m E7 E♭7(♭13) A♭6 G⌀7 C7(♭9)
42 Fm B♭7 E♭m A♭7(♭9)
46 D♭m B♭⌀7 E♭7(♭9) A♭m6 E7 A7 D7 G7 C7 F7 B♭7 E♭7
51 A♭6 G♭7(♯11) C⌀7 F7(♭9) B♭m7 E♭7
55 E♭m7 B♭7(♯9) E♭m7 A♭7(♭9) D♭6 A♭m7 D♭7
59 G♭maj7 C⌀7 F7(♭9) B♭m7 E♭7(♯11) D♭7(♯5)
63 Cm7 F7 B♭m7 F7 B♭7 E♭7 A♭6 E♭7

67
Ab6
Gb7(#11)
Cø7
F7(b9)
Bbm7
I ain't got no death wish, I'm not per-verse
I'm sim-ply ter-ri-fied of

71
Eb7(#11)
Bbm
E7
Eb7(b13)
a - ging. And af - ter the fort - 'eth "fete de la birth,"

74
Ab6
Gø7
C7(b9)
Fm
3
the bo-dy's ba-sic-ally de - cay - ing. Years pass us

77
Bb7
3
Ebm
3
Ab7(b9)
by, yet goals stay un - met. Time fills with meals to cook and clothes to laun-der

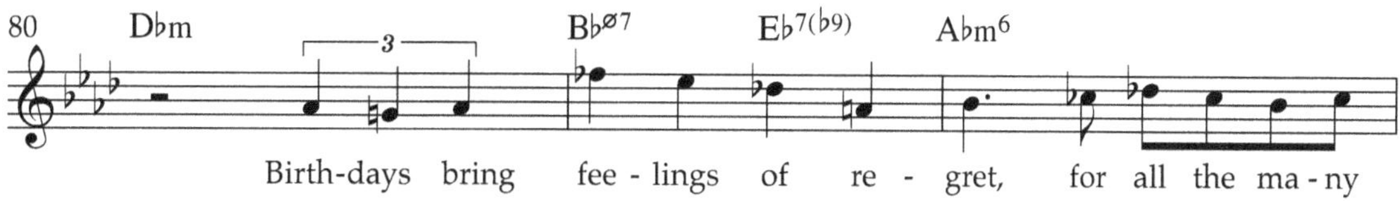
80
Dbm
3
Bbø7
Eb7(b9)
Abm6
Birth-days bring fee - lings of re - gret, for all the ma - ny

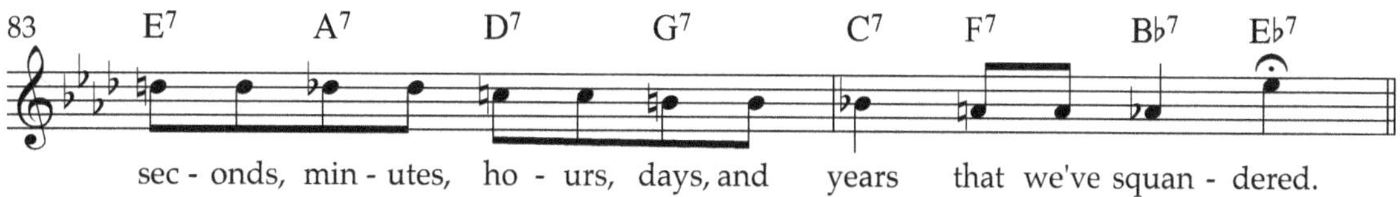
83
E7
A7
D7
G7
C7
F7
Bb7
Eb7
sec - onds, min - utes, ho - urs, days, and years that we've squan - dered.

85
A♭6
G♭7(♯11)
C⌀7
F7(♭9)
B♭m7
Is - n't it sil - ly to come un - done, just 'cause it's some day in Oc -

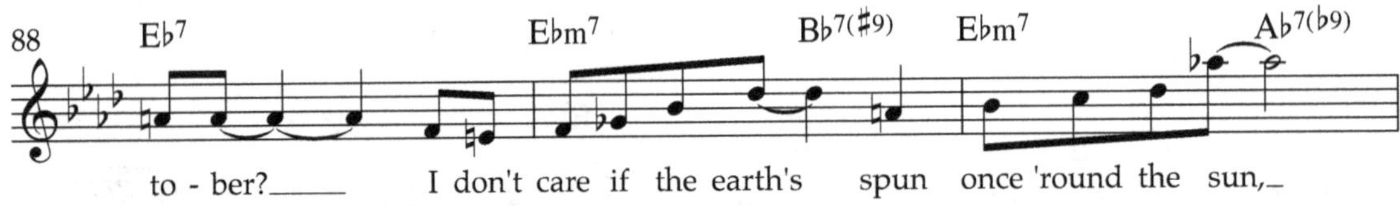
88
E♭7
E♭m7
B♭7(♯9)
E♭m7
A♭7(♭9)
to - ber? I don't care if the earth's spun once 'round the sun,

91
D♭6
A♭m7
D♭7
G♭maj7
Yet I can't face this mo-ment so - ber. I know that I

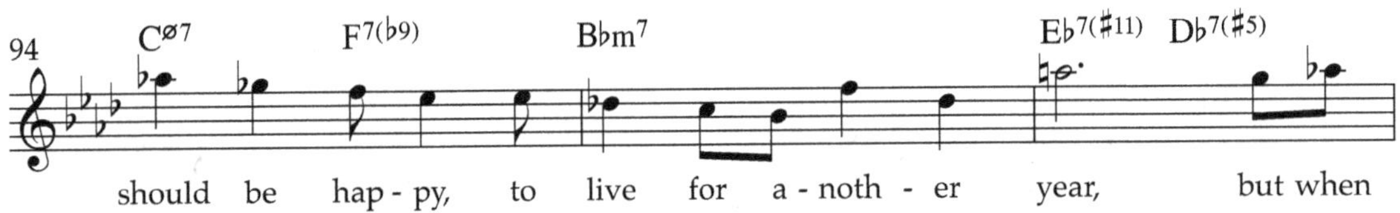
94
C⌀7
F7(♭9)
B♭m7
E♭7(♯11)
D♭7(♯5)
should be hap - py, to live for a - noth - er year, but when

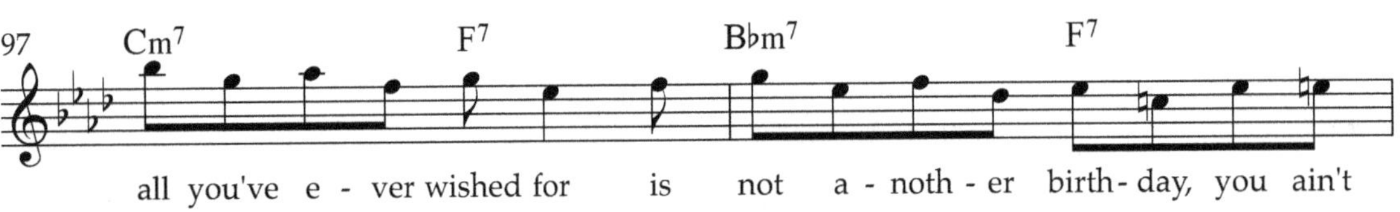
97
Cm7
F7
B♭m7
F7
all you've e - ver wished for is not a - noth - er birth- day, you ain't

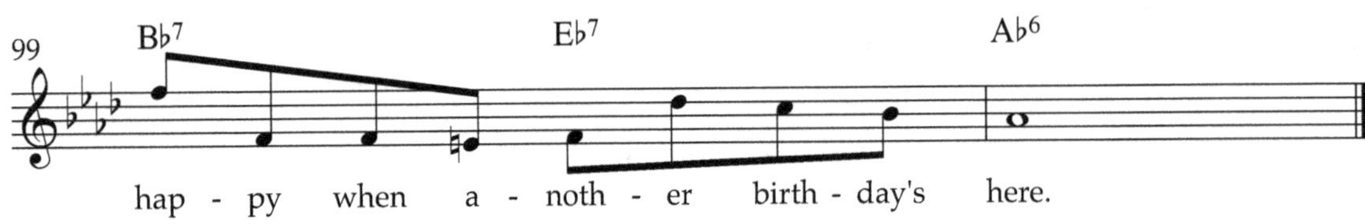
99
B♭7
E♭7
A♭6
hap - py when a - noth - er birth - day's here.

Lyrics

I'd Given Up
I'd given up on the power of art
To change a life.
But there you were,
Real as an angel,
Doing it to me. (4x)

Unbroken String
Had my heart an unbroken string,
Your touch would set it trembling.
Though music left me long ago,
My song could still be sweet.
One touch would set me trembling,
And start my heart to beat.

Had my heart an unclipped wing,
Your smile would start it fluttering.
Though I was grounded long ago,
I dream of open sky.
Your smile could mend my broken wings,
One smile and I could fly.

Had my heart a sturdy oar,
Your kiss would launch me from the shore.
Though I've been landlocked 'lo these years,
I crave the ocean's spray.
If you kissed me, dear,
My heart could sail away.

In Every Moment
Hold me this midwinter's night.
Even lilac trees wear their wedding gowns.
Time doesn't exist.
For as we kiss, the seconds breed perpetual infinities.
Our souls were born to harmonize eternally.
I will die into your arms this night
With faith I'll feel the sun as it shines out your soul.
I know I will.
Our lives begin with suicide,
Embrace me and be born again in showers of turquoise and gold.
Die into me now, my love.

I'd Break Quarantine for You, Verse 1
I'd break quarantine for you, my love.
You're the only dream I'm dreaming of.
Folks in government may disagree,
but you're the medicine for me.

Your kiss is electric,
Makes me weak in the knees,
If your love is infectious, dear,
I want the disease.

'Cause you're a living, breathing dream come true,
I'd break quarantine for you.

Lethe-Reincarnation
I remember waking up on Sundays.
Sunlight streaking softly through the blinds.
Mother's voice is calling from the pantry.
Take this memory and give me life.

Biking up the hill along the train tracks.
Clouds are painted pink with evening's light.
Friends are laughing with the joy of summer.

I remember meeting him that winter.
Glimpsing something special in his eyes.
Ev'ry word he spoke sounded like music
Take this memory and give me life.

Drinking Song
I never had a taste for cold humanity.
People are so stuffy.
They're always workin' at a job all day.
Waitin' for the weekend

But when you drink it yanks you out of your body.
And that shoddy day today.
Ev'ry low-life gets a chance at a new life,
When toasting "to life," living fades away...

Aviator gin can make a sad man soar
Up among the barflies.
So leave your worldly troubles at the tavern door.
That humdrum stuff can't touch you anymore.
One more pour!

Serotiny
Bless this land,
This land that burns itself to dust each year.
The smoking sea attends by candle light,
As wooded worlds ignite.
The flames proclaim the gospel,
The wind, like an apostle, sends ash misting down like desert rain.

Release your seeds.
The sprouts and flowers will be hatched of heat.
And let the red moon shed tears
There's no grief without growth
And no love without grief.

I'd Break Quarantine for You, Verse 2
I'd break quarantine for you, my sweet.
Without you next to me,
I'm incomplete.
Experts ev'rywhere say stay inside,
But what I feel can't be denied.

Leaving home is a "no-no," but I long for your touch.
Surely governor Cuomo wouldn't mind it too much...

If sweethearts reconvene a rendezvous,
I'd break quarantine for you.

Kneel
When the body cannot bear it,
when the pity's too profound,
When mem'ries break like waves against your conscience,
Kneel your knees upon the ground.

Weep for emptiness and fullness,
Cry for pebbles and for clouds,
For curling smoke above forgotten houses,
Kneel your knees upon the ground.

A schoolgirl in blue and white,
Whirling in evening's light,
A kiss by the boathouse door leaving you needing more,
The horns of the harbor heard chanting love, word by word,
To live it is raw and rare,
Like a prayer, ev'rywhere.

Feel the soil soft beneath you,
See the hills in ochre drowned,
And hear the bugle-colored twilight blowing,
Kneel your knees upon the ground.

So, I Went to New York City
And so I went to New York City to be born again
And be delivered by the snarl of crowds.
That picket fence life was a practice trial,
So rob me or cheat me,
I know in my soul, I'm alive.

And so I camped out for the evening down in Battery Park.
That night I vowed to search for love on ev'ry avenue
And great ev'ry sunrise with a newborn's smile.
Starlight above me whispered, "You're alive."

Let this be my epitaph:
"Her soul was born to fly."
Let the small town critics laugh.
But I ain't afraid of,
I'm not afraid of,
I'm not afraid of open skies.
And so I went to New York City to be born again.

And so I went to New York City to become brand new.
And I was baptized by the Hudson's spray.
My soul awoke to hear a vendor's cry.
His voice was like music,
The melody said, "you're alive!"
Fill my soul with energy.
Make me a neon sign.
When the crowds remember me,
They'll say I was born to,
Say I was born to,
Say I was born to brightly shine.
And so I went to New York City to be born again.

New
I'm nervous, I'm restless, I'm all short of breath.
I'm electric, elated, But scared half to death.
Though I've known heartache and dark nights,
I'm catchin' glimses of new light,
A shimmer, a sparkle, a flicker, a star.

Could it be that I'm in love again?
Could I set my heart loose
'though it's battered and bruised?
I crave that love that never ends,
So I'll tell you my secrets and hold you 'til night turns to morn.

While the sun warms the fallow fields,
And sets all the flow'rs in bloom,
Love me and make me new.

We Will Not Go Back to Normal
Take a breath, close your eyes,
Take my hand, hold it tight.
Take the time to free your mind and dream.
Dream of love, in bloom like lilac trees.
Dream of love, of reawakening.

We've seen the hoarding, hating, suff'ring, raging,
Normalized greed,
Friends, let us seek new ways to be.

Take a breath, in, then out.
Take the time to be here now.
Now we're called to heal our hurt,
So let's make the healing
Glorious, magnificent,
And let us not return, not rewind,
Not repeat, revert,

Reach out your hand, take hold of mine.
Understand, together, we can make this right.
Let this be our prayer,
Help us love others, Lord.
Let this be our prayer,
Hlp us to love ourselves too.
Let's make it new.

Take my hand, hold it tight,
take a breath, close your eyes.
Take the time to free your mind and dream.
Dream a dream of what the spring could be.
Let this be our prayer,
Help us love others, Lord.
Let this be our prayer,
Help us to love ourselves too.
Help us, Lord, to make it new.

Growing Pains
(no lyric)

I'd Break Quarantine for You, Verse 3
I'd break quarantine for you, my pet!
Laws can't come between our sweet duet.
Coughs and sniffles won't deter my, dear,
For true love always conquers fear.

I wither without you here,
I miss you to death.
When I daydream about you, dear,
I get short of breath...

So let's convene a social call for two,
I'd break quarantine for you.

Long Beach, In Fog
Listening, listening,
It's still in the street.
Silently disappear,
Listening.

Closing your eyes,
Fade into mist,
Vanish slowly.

Wandering, wandering,
Deep in the ocean's breath.
Ghosts slowly pirouette,
Listening.

New Year, New You
"New Year, New You."
Not real, ain't true.
No calendar change is gonna change who you see in the mirror.
New year, new goals.
That shit gets old.
Nom you can't change anything that's deep down
'Cause of some countdown.

We all wish we could shed our skin like a snake.
Brother it ain't that simple.
Real change is like trudging through mud for miles.
Real change ain't like popping a pimple.

"New Year, New You."
Not real, ain't true.
New year, be bold.
It all makes me feels old.

They say change arrives like the drop of a hat.
Real life ain't so fickle.
This day ain't the first of the rest of your life.
It's just one more day in the middle.

"New Year, New You."
Not real, ain't true.
New year, can't lie.
Each year, I still try.

I'd Break Quarantine for You, Verse 4
I broke quarantine for you, for you,
To hold you, darling, was a dream come true.
To kiss you on the lips was my life's thrill,
But then I started feeling ill.

My whole body's congested, twice as bad as the flu.
I'm about to get tested and I think you should too.

I'm feeble, feverish, and feeling blue.
'Cause I broke quarantine for you.

April, the Liar
Beauty, can bloom in the meadow of youth.
Fresh love is glor'ous when it's new.
Springtime brings promises of thrills renewed, dreams revived,
But, in truth it's April again.
And I feel all the frosts of age.
'Though daffodils are lovely, don't be fooled,
No flower brings perennial youth.
We're all gonna die.
April's a lie.

Demeter
The stone room echoes my half-formed words.
The cold air cuts like a dagger.
My soul is as cold as the primal earth,
for Hades has stolen my daughter.

Sleep, oh Sleep, engulf me now.
Bring me dreams of fields and flow'rs.
My daughter paints the fields and the flow'rs,
But my daughter's been stolen away.
And the fields are just dirt, dust, and clay.

I'd Break Quarantine for You, Verse 5
I broke quarantine for you, for you.
Then an unforeseen event ensued.
At the hospital, your breathing failed
'Til you finally exhaled.

Oh my darling I miss you, now I feel so alone.
Sure, I shouldn't have kissed you, then, but who could have known?

Dear, love seemed evergreen and worry free,
When you broke quarantine for me.

Forgiveness
I thought I saw your face,
When I passed by the school today.
Can you forgive me, my friend?
Forgive me, forgive me, we were kids back then.

I wrote to you last year
And I made my apology.
I should have sent it long ago.
You must have felt so alone, but you should know

When I'm on the train,
I watch the years roll by like endless hills.
'Though you and I have traveled diff'rent tracks,
I think about you still.

I wake to morning sun,
And once more realize you're gone.
Can you forgive me, my friend?

Another Birthday

Blow out the candles, make a wish.
I wish for not another birthday.
Invite all your friends and make believe,
Pretend it's not another birthday.
Wrinkles my deepen, and hairs may turn gray.
New weight will appear in the midsection,
One hardly needs a special day
To be reminded time only runs in one direction.

Open the presents, sing the song,
The whole occassion feels so childish.
Be a good sport and play along.
Honor this day you turn senilish.
Sure I'm lucky to be toasted yearly by family and friends,
But the next time that we gather to toast another birthday,
I hope the birthday boy is one of them.

I ain't got no death wish, I'm not perverse,
I'm simply terrified of aging.
And after the fort'eth "fete de la birth,"
The body's basically decaying.
Years pass us by, yet goals stay unmet.
Time fills with meals to cook and clothes to launder,
Birthdays bring feelings of regret,
For all the many seconds, minutes, hours, days, and years that we've squandered.

Isn't it silly to come undone,
Just 'cause it's some day in October?
I don't care if the earth's spun once 'round the sun,
Yet I can't face this moment sober.
I know that I should be happy, to live for another year,
But when all you've ever wished for is not another birthday,
You ain't happy when another birthday's here.

Selected Transcriptions

Drinking Song

Piano Solo by Jeremy Siskind

(8)
13 Cm
E7
Bmaj7
3
3
straight
swung
16 D7(♭9)
G7(♯9)
A♭7
D♭7
F♯7
B7
3
3
19 E7(♭9)
A7
F♯7
B♭7
B7
E
3
straight
swung
22 A7
Fm
3
3
3
25 E7
Am
B♭7
3
3
3

27
A7
D7
G7(♭9)
C7
29
A7
D♭7
F♯7
B
31
D♭7(♭9)
C7
F7
8vb
34
B♭7
E♭
D7(♭9)
37
D♭7
D♭o7
Cm
E7

39 Bmaj7
D7(♭9)
G7(♯9)
42 A♭7
D♭7
F♯7
B7
E7(♭9)
A7
F♯7
B♭7
B7
E
A7
45
48
Fm
50 E7
Am
B♭7
A7

Forgiveness

Solo by Jeremy Siskind

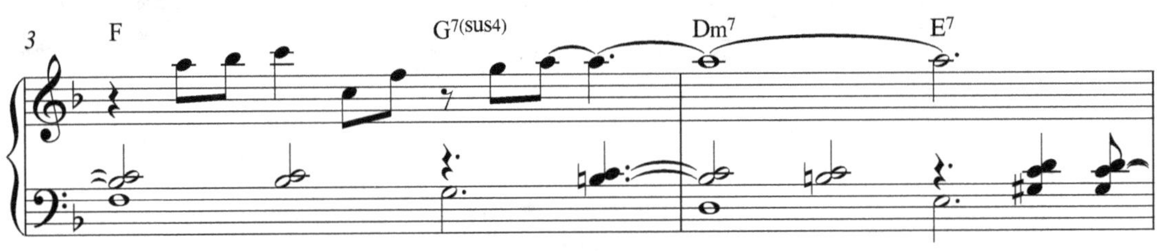

9
F
Gm11
B♭/D
C/D

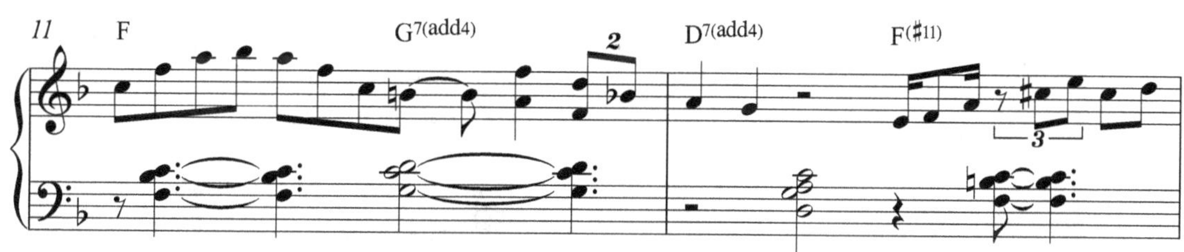
11
F
G7(add4)
2
D7(add4)
F(♯11)
3

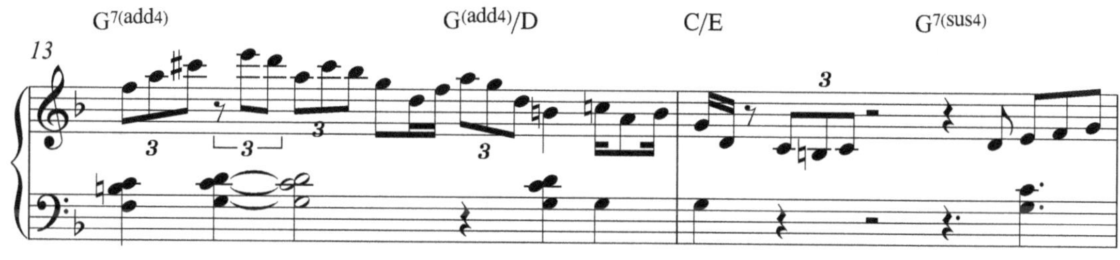
13
G7(add4)
G(add4)/D
C/E
G7(sus4)
3

15
D7(♯11)
E+
G7(sus4)
D7(♯11)

17
C♯m
F♯(add4)
A(♯4)
3

19
Bm7
F♯m7(♭6)
21
Fmaj7
E+
Dm7
23
Gm7
C7(sus4)

New Year, New You

Solos by Lucas Pino (saxophone) and Jeremy Siskind (piano)

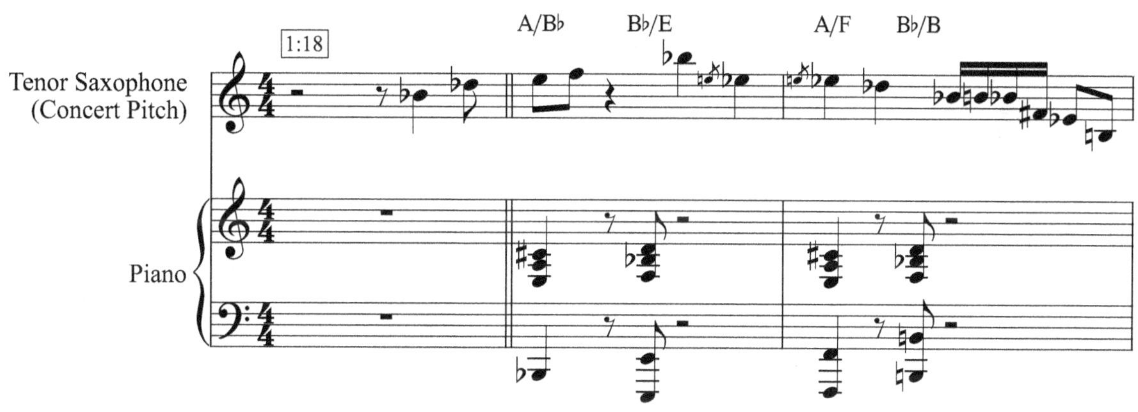

8
Ten. Sax.
3
Pno.

10
A/B♭
B♭/E
A/F
B♭/B
3
F♯m/B♭
E♭/D
Pno.

13
D/A♭
G♭/C
F♯7
Pno.

16
B♭m
B♭+7
Pno.

19
Ten. Sax.
3
3
3
Pno.
3
20
E7alt.
3
F7alt.
3
3
Ten. Sax.
Pno.
21
E7alt.
F7alt.
Ten. Sax.
Pno.
22
E7alt.
3
F7alt.
3
3
3
Ten. Sax.
Pno.

23
E7alt.
F7alt.
A7alt.
B♭7alt.
Ten. Sax.
Pno.
25
A7alt.
B♭7alt.
3
Ten. Sax.
Pno.
26
A7alt.
B♭7alt.
A7alt.
A♭7alt.
3
Ten. Sax.
Pno.
3
28
Gm(maj7)
C7(♯11)
Gm(maj7)
C7(♯11)
A♭m(maj7)
D♭7(♯11)
3
3
Pno.

31 A♭m(maj7)
D♭7(♯11)
F♯
C
Pno.

33
F♯
C
G♭/G
D/A♭
A/B♭
Pno.

36
Interlude
Pno.

38
A/B♭
B♭/E
Ten. Sax.
Pno.

40
A/F
B♭/B
Ten. Sax.
Pno.
41
F♯m/B♭
5
B♭/F♯
Ten. Sax.
Pno.
42
F/D
F♯/A
3
Ten. Sax.
Pno.
43
A/F♯
D♭/B
3
5
Ten. Sax.
Pno.

44
B♭/E
E♭/D♭
B♭+/E♭
B/G
A/F
B♭
Ten. Sax.
Pno.
47
A/B♭
B♭/E
A/F
B♭/B
Pno.
49
F♯m/B♭
B♭/F♯
F/D
F♯/A
Pno.
51
E♭7
Ten. Sax.
Pno.

53
Ten. Sax.
Pno.
55 A/B♭
B♭/E
A/F
B♭/B
57
F♯m/B♭
E♭/D
D/A♭
G♭/C
59 F♯7

61
B♭m
Ten. Sax.
3
3
Pno.
63
B♭+7
Ten. Sax.
3
Pno.

Unbroken String

Piano Solo by Jeremy Siskind

33
G♭maj7/B♭
Gmaj7/B
Dm7
3
3
36
3
3
Amaj7
A♭/C
39
G♭(sus4)
A♭/C
B♭/D
Amaj7
43
D♭maj7
E♭(sus4)
G7(sus4)
Cmaj7
47
E♭m7
F7(♭9)
E♭/G
50
A♭7(sus4)
A°7
B♭m
Gm7
53
Dmaj7(♯11)
(tenths)
G♭maj7/B♭
Gmaj7/B
3
3
57
Dm7
Amaj7
A♭/C
G♭(sus4)

www.ingramcontent.com/pod-product-compliance
Lightning Source LLC
Chambersburg PA
CBHW081255040426
42452CB00014B/2508
* 9 7 8 1 7 3 5 1 6 9 5 6 9 *